INTERVIEWING
FOR MANAGERS

INTERVIEWING FOR MANAGERS

A COMPLETE GUIDE TO EMPLOYMENT INTERVIEWING

John D. Drake

Revised Edition

amacom

A DIVISION OF AMERICAN MANAGEMENT ASSOCIATIONS

Library of Congress Cataloging in Publication Data

Drake, John D., 1928–
    Interviewing for managers.

    Bibliography: p. 265
    Includes index.
    1. Employment interviewing. I. Title.
HF5549.5.I6D7   1982   658.3'1124   81-69360
ISBN 0-8144-5737-1   AACR2

First Printing

For my wife, Delia,
who makes life beautiful and exciting

Preface

The revised edition of *Interviewing for Managers,* like its predecessor, is a how-to book to help managers more effectively evaluate job candidates. The original text was rewritten for a number of reasons. I have had an additional ten years' experience in working with clients who are applying the techniques and principles described in the first edition. This hands-on exposure has enabled me to observe new ways in which the methodologies and techniques can be refined and made more applicable for nonprofessional interviewers. An example is the two-on-one interview. Many clients have adopted this method to reduce the number of interviews per applicant and, at the same time, increase their predictive accuracy. This edition gives more attention to the conduct and structuring of these interviews.

A second major change has occurred in the area of equal employment opportunity. At the time the original edition was written in 1972, the concept of women as a "minority" in the marketplace was unrecognized. The first book primarily focused on the role of male as interviewer and male as applicant for key positions. This revised edition focuses on techniques for evaluating *persons,* not males or females. Also, a new chapter has been added that discusses equal employment regulations and the selection process.

A third reason for revising the book was to make it a more complete compendium for the selection-interview process. In the new edition, therefore, chapters have been added about finding candidates. Obviously the value of any selection technique, such as interviewing, is only as good as the quality and variety of candidates being considered. Thus, new chapters deal with recruiting personnel from both the college campus and the general job market. Another new chapter describes a process for selling the applicant. It focuses on a problem many organizations face—recruiting people to unattractive locations and/or industries that are not currently popular or in vogue. The procedures described have been successfully employed by many organizations and should be helpful to managers in selling the company, job, and location.

What makes this book unique is that it presents a technique, the hypothesis method, that provides help in evaluating data. This is the most difficult problem faced by all interviewers—how to put meaning on what is heard. This technique provides a clear-cut methodology for conducting the interview. Thus, this book presents an integrated system for interviewing, a system that achieves the greatest yield of helpful information per minute of time.

Most of the material in this book is based on my experiences with clients in recruiting, selecting, and making hiring decisions. It is a compilation of one consultant's view of what is practical and effective in the hiring of personnel.

I want to acknowledge the contribution of Robert De-Largey, senior vice-president and manager of the Houston office of Drake Beam Morin, Inc., whose firsthand experiences provided substantial material for Chapter 10, "Selling the Candidate—Managing the Visit." John Ryan, director of personnel, Schering-Plough, also contributed significantly from his experiences with job posting. I also wish to acknowledge the patience and efforts of my typist, Marilyn Giles.

John D. Drake

Contents

     Appendix A   A List of Tested Questions   249

     Appendix B   Interviewer's Feedback
                  Checklist   257

     Appendix C   Developing Behavioral Specifi-
                  cations   259

     Appendix D   Suggested Agenda for a Two-
                  Day College Recruiter Work-
                  shop   262

     Appendix E   A Sample Format for Request-
                  ing Transcripts   264

     Selected Reading   265

     Index   267

CHAPTER 1

The Interview as an Assessment Tool

Anyone who works in contact with others assesses others. The salesman assesses the sales prospect to determine his approach; the manager evaluates the capabilities of his subordinate before giving him a critical assignment. Unfortunately, most assessing is done rather haphazardly—without much system or plan. Observation of behavior, prior "track records," verbal comments, and out-and-out hunches are often combined in some random manner to help arrive at personnel decisions.

While data from each of these sources can be helpful in evaluating others, the vehicle that is the most readily available, and at the same time permits the integration of many sources of information, is the interview. All of us continually judge others—by what they say, how they express themselves, and what they tell us about themselves. Sometimes we are quite effective in evaluating others by their verbal comments; more often we err. The following segment of an interview, taken from an actual tape recording, illustrates the point.

INTERVIEWER: I see [referring to an application blank] that you went to Rutgers University.
APPLICANT: That's right. I got my bachelor's there last year.

1

INTERVIEWER: How'd you like it?

APPLICANT: Oh, it was fine—it's a good school and it prepared me well for graduate work.

INTERVIEWER: Yes, I see here that you went on to NYU. That was when you were working for the Robinson Company. Did you go in the evenings?

APPLICANT: That's right. I took two courses each semester. It takes a while to get your degree at nights, but the instructors are very good.

INTERVIEWER: You know, we're interested in fellows who are willing to work hard to get ahead—people who don't mind getting their hands dirty. Incidentally, when you are out on calls with customers, how would you feel about having to lift cartons and packing cases once in a while?

APPLICANT: Well, I've always had to work hard, but are you telling me that even as a college grad I'm going to have to do manual labor?

INTERVIEWER: Don't worry about that. You'll be moving along quite quickly into a supervisory assignment, and that will be the end of it. You know, when I started with the company six years ago, why we had to. . . .

On this tape the interviewer was trying his best. Time was passing, dialog was taking place, but the amount of helpful information he was eliciting was negligible. Even if the interview continued, there was little likelihood that the interviewer would acquire a clear understanding of how the candidate would perform on the job.

What else could the interviewer have done? Ideally, he could have said less. Instead of talking so much, he might have asked more penetrating questions and not have inquired about information that was already available to him from the application blank. He might have asked questions that would have given him some insight into how the applicant behaves rather than what he did. In the dialog quoted, an opportunity was created by the interviewer to learn about the candidate's attitude toward manual labor. In this instance, the interviewer could have encouraged discussion of the topic, without putting the candidate on the spot, by conveying an understanding of the applicant's viewpoint. For example, the interviewer could have said, "In view of your education, you feel it would be a bit beneath you to get involved in any manual work."

The interviewer's reflection of the applicant's statement invites the applicant to elaborate on his attitudes and values. In this way, with the candidate thinking out loud about his own feelings, both the applicant and the interviewer can learn more about how the candidate is likely to react to the requirements of the job.

In the following account on the same general topic, we can see the results of these principles at work.

INTERVIEWER: Tell me a little bit about your career there at Rutgers.

APPLICANT: I'm not exactly sure what you want. Should I talk about my grades or what?

INTERVIEWER: Oh, I had nothing particular in mind— whatever you think would be helpful for me to know.

APPLICANT: Well, I felt that Rutgers was a good school—a bit tough, but I learned a lot even though my grades suffered a bit during my last two years. As far as sports go, I was on the tennis team and played intramurals, you know— baseball and basketball. I was also quite active in my fraternity, and was rush committee chairman in my junior year. I also was the treasurer. I don't know what else to say. I liked the school and enjoyed myself socially.

INTERVIEWER: You mentioned that your grades dropped a bit during your last two years. What might be some of the factors that accounted for that?

APPLICANT: Well, I didn't fail anything, but I had quite a few D's. I guess that I just played too much.

INTERVIEWER: You put more time into the social activities than you should have.

APPLICANT: Well, I didn't exactly stop studying, but I guess I was trying to do too much. I think I was applying myself as hard as ever, but I just couldn't keep burning the candle at both ends. [Pause] I guess I'm best when I'm doing one thing at a time.

INTERVIEWER: You don't seem to be as efficient if you have to juggle a lot of balls at the same time.

APPLICANT: Yeah, I guess that's it. I know that when I was in graduate school I concentrated on. . . .

In the second interview, we can see immediately that the applicant is doing most of the talking. Not only did the interviewer learn about the poor grades and extracurricular activities, but, more important, the interviewer is beginning to gain some understanding of how this person behaves at work. He has been told that the candidate is probably at his best when handling one thing at a time. At this stage in the interview, the statement can be regarded only as a hypothesis. However, if the same trait manifests itself at other times in the applicant's life history, it becomes a meaningful input for the interviewer—particularly if the job for which the applicant is being considered requires him to keep many different activities going simultaneously.

To carry out the analysis described here, it is not essential for the interviewer to have psychological or personnel training. The necessary raw materials for being a good judge of others are reasonable intelligence and a sensitivity or "feel" for others.

Because it is almost axiomatic that the success of any manager depends upon the depth of talent with which he surrounds himself, it becomes absolutely critical for him to learn to effectively evaluate manpower. The interview is one tool he can use and one he can learn to use well. But first, let us examine how effective the interview is as a tool for assessing others.

How Good Is the Interview as an Assessment Tool?

Until recently, much of the research concerning the effectiveness of the interview for predicting job behavior has shown disappointing results. Investigators often found little relationship between the ratings generated by interviewers and actual on-the-job performance. It is interesting to note, however, that most of the researchers did not concern themselves with the skills of the interviewers. In fact, in many studies in which the interview turned out to be a relatively ineffective assessment device, the interviewers were not particularly well trained. And even in those studies that reported the interviewers to have had some fundamental interview training, the interviewers were rarely required to follow a specified technique or procedure. It is not surprising, therefore, that many of the studies showed the interview to be a rather limited tool for assessing others. By contrast, when an experienced, skillful interviewer makes an assessment, he can demonstrate good predictive accuracy.[1]

Because the available research data seem to be ambiguous and at times conflicting, the author conducted two studies to help clarify the issues. These research projects were designed to compare the effectiveness of interviewers before and after training. They represent an attempt to ascertain if nonprofessional interviewers (operating managers) can learn and apply specific interview procedures. If the participant can apply the techniques successfully, then the value of the interview as a tool for managers can be demonstrated. Furthermore, if managers learn to use particular techniques and if they are effective, then certain predictable results should occur.

□ The trained interviewers should be consistent with one another in their judgments—at least mor consistent than when judgments are rendered by untrained interviewers.

□ Trained interviewers should have a good "batting average" in evaluating candidates. The accuracy of their predictions should be higher than the accuracy of those who are untrained.

An Experiment in Consistency

In the first study, the research was designed to ascertain whether or not those trained in interviewing were more consistent with each other in their evaluations than those not trained. In this project, two different adult college classes

[1] E. E. Ghiselli, "The Validity of a Personnel Interview," *Personnel Psychology*, No. 4, 1966, pp. 389–394.

were exposed to a brief résumé and a fifty-minute tape recording of an interview. This tape was made during an actual interview that had been conducted by the author. The applicant was a twenty-four-year-old male candidate for a sales representative job with a large consumer marketing company. The classes were approximately the same size and were comprised largely of middle management business and professional men attending evening university courses in business subjects. The students in Class I were enrolled in a course on interviewing. Of the thirty-eight members of this class, only five were employed in personnel departments or had extensive interviewing experience prior to attending the class. Class II was comprised of a similar group of business and professional personnel. These men and women had signed up for a course in personnel administration.

Both classes were independently exposed to the résumé and the tape recording. Each student was also given a job description of the sales representative position. The students in each class were asked to evaluate the qualifications of the candidate for the sales representative job on a seven-point scale.

The findings of this study were most interesting. Before training, both Class I and Class II were approximately equal in how they evaluated the candidate. That is, the mean rating of the students in Class I was 4.6 (average to above average), while the mean for Class II was 4.8. Both classes were also approximately the same in the extent to which their respective raters differed in their opinions. The more the ratings cluster around the mean, the more consistent, of course, are the ratings. For the two classes studied, the standard devia-

Point Value	Description
7	Superior
6	Above average
5	Average to above average
4	Average
3	Average to below average
2	Below average
1	Poor

tion (SD) provides an index of the range of scores. The higher the SD, the more the majority of the raters vary from the mean. As can be noted in Figure 1, the SD for both classes was approximately equal, 3.1 and 2.8, respectively. Thus it can be said that both classes were basically equal in their assessment capabilities.

Six weeks after the first evaluations, the same tape and résumé were provided for a second time to both classes. In the interval, Class I was trained in the interview techniques described in this book; Class II continued its regular studies in personnel administration (not including interviewing). Notice the column headed "Second Interview" in Figure 1. For Class I, the interview-trained class, the range of ratings decreased from 3.1 to 1.2. This finding shows a marked increase in intrarater consistency between the first and second interviews. For Class II, however, the noninterview-trained group, the variability remained high at 2.9. The likelihood of such a difference occurring between Class I and Class II as a result of chance is less than one in a hundred. It is quite evident, therefore, that those trained in the interview techniques were more consistent in their ratings than those who were untrained.

It is interesting to note the differences in mean (average scores) obtained by the two classes. After listening to the tape for a second time, members of Class I were much more critical in their ratings of the candidate than before the training. In other words, after interview training, the Class I students not only agreed more consistently with each other but they also tended to view the candidate as less well qualified than on the first assessment. For Class II students, on the other

FIGURE 1. *Comparison of the variability of ratings for groups trained and not trained in interview techniques.*

Class	Measure	First Interview	Interviewer Trained	Second Interview	Interviewer Trained
I $N=38$	Mean Rating Range (SD)	4.6 3.1	No	3.4 1.2	Yes
II $N=31$	Mean Rating Range (SD)	4.8 2.8	No	4.5 2.9	No

hand, consistency and qualifications ratings were almost the same for the second interview as for the first.

An Experiment in Predictability

A second study was conducted to determine how accurate the interview might be as a tool for predicting on-the-job performance. In this instance, an attempt was also made to evaluate the effectiveness of the techniques outlined in this book.

The situation that permitted the study was the acquisition by a major chemical corporation of a smaller high-technology company. Many of the acquired firm's manufacturing and research facilities were to be integrated into an already existing division of the chemical firm. Because it was necessary to merge the manpower of the two groups, an evaluation of managerial and professional talents had to be made in the acquired firm. To accomplish the assessment, two teams of five men were selected to interview the personnel. These interviewers were—with the exception of one man in each team—operating managerial personnel with strong chemical engineering backgrounds. (Technical sophistication

Points	Descriptive Rating	Qualifiable Job Level
6	Extraordinary managerial talent—ready for top-echelon management	Division Head
5	Very good managerial talent—ready for upper middle management	Department Head
4	Good managerial talent—ready for middle management assignment	Section Head
3	Good in managerial talent—ready for supervisory level assignment	Supervisor
2	Fair managerial talent—marginally effective at directing others	_____
1	Poor—limited skill for a supervisory assignment	_____

was thought to be an important ingredient in establishing rapport and meaningful communication between the interviewers and the acquired company's staff.) Each of the teams included a personnel department representative who had extensive interviewing experience.

In conducting the evaluation interviews, the teams followed no consistent pattern. Sometimes two or three members of the team would jointly interview a candidate; sometimes the interviews were conducted on a one-to-one basis. However, for each candidate assessed, the members of the interviewing team met as a group and arrived at some composite evaluation. For these evaluations, a six-point scale of management acceptability was used.

In the first round of assessments, sixty-six males were evaluated. The evaluation ratings were then correlated with the acquired company's performance ratings from the prior three years. As Figure 2 shows, the correlation of the evaluation ratings of the two groups with job-rated performances was low: .25 and .22, respectively. Because it had been anticipated that a much higher degree of concurrence would be found between prior performance records and the team assessments, the author was authorized to train one of the interviewing teams. The situation represented a unique opportunity to put the trained-interviewer theory to a test.

In this research project, Team A was trained; Team B was not. After Team A was given three days of training, a second round of evaluations was begun. This time, 104 people (99

FIGURE 2.   *Effect of interview training on predictive accuracy of interviewers.*

Team	Number Evaluated	First Round Assessments	Interviewers Trained	Number Evaluated	Second Round Assessments	Interviewers Trained
A	31	.25*	No	54	.44*	Yes
B	35	.22*	No	50	.26*	No

*Indicates correlations between interview ratings and management performance ratings.

males; 5 females) were assessed. The results were exciting. As can be seen in Figure 2, Team A almost doubled its predictive accuracy, while the untrained team remained at approximately the same level. Here was convincing evidence of the greater consistency and validity of the ratings of those trained in interviewing techniques. The findings demonstrate, too, that in a relatively short period of time managers can learn to predict, with reasonable accuracy, on-the-job performance.

It now seems increasingly evident that simply sitting down and talking with candidates about themselves or their qualifications is not likely to produce consistent or valid findings. An interviewer needs to follow procedures that have been tested and proved effective. This book describes one such set of techniques or procedures. They need not be slavishly followed but rather adapted to the interviewer's own personality and the circumstances of the interview. It is important, however, that certain fundamental principles be adhered to and certain procedural steps followed. In subsequent chapters, a clear step-by-step method is described. The approach should lend itself well to many different kinds of interviews, although it is geared, essentially, to helping executivies make hire, not-hire decisions about job applicants and candidates for promotion.

Summary

The interview is the most convenient vehicle for evaluating others. However, until recently, much of the research concerning the effectiveness of the interview for predicting job behavior has shown disappointing results, possibly because the researchers did not concern themselves with the skills of the interviewers. More recent research indicates that predictive accuracy improves sharply when managers are trained in the interviewing techniques outlined in this book.

CHAPTER 2

Problems in Interviewing

Before embarking on a study of the techniques and procedures that can make interviewing effective, we should first pinpoint the difficulties we are most likely to encounter in interviewing—the kinds of problems that get in the way of effective assessment. Once these obstacles have been identified, the procedures described in this book will become quite meaningful because they were specifically designed to overcome these difficulties, which all of us encounter when evaluating others.

The problems depicted in this chapter were gleaned from an analysis of more than 500 tape recordings of employment interviews. These interviews were conducted both by managers who had little interviewing experience and by professional interviewers. An interesting finding was that the professional interviewers made the same basic mistakes as the amateurs. You will probably identify your own errors among the most frequently observed mistakes.

- □ Talking too much; we don't listen enough.
- □ Jumping to conclusions.
- □ "Telegraphing" the desired responses to our questions.
- □ Failing to translate data about past behavior to on-the-job performance.

Let us examine each of these areas of difficulty in more detail.

Talking Too Much

By far the most common error encountered in interviewing is a tendency for the interviewer to dominate the conversation. This occurs for many reasons. Many managers achieve their positions of leadership, in part, because they have good verbal skills. They find little difficulty in expressing themselves and they usually enjoy communicating. Thus, it is more natural for them to verbalize and dominate the discussion than to be quiet and listen.

A second reason many managers talk too much in interview situations is that they feel more comfortable when they are in control and in command. They wish to avoid the discomfort of silence or the awkwardness of trying to get the candidate to talk about a topic that puts managers on unfamiliar ground. Consequently, they discuss subjects about which they are knowledgeable (the company, the industry, or themselves), but tend to avoid the unknown—the applicant sitting across from them.

A third factor that gets in the way of listening is that some output and communication from the interviewer is both expected and desired. After all, there is a need to ask questions, explain about the job, sell the applicant on the company, and even engage in some relaxing small talk. However, the problem is one of balance; in a high proportion of interviews, there is far too much telling and not enough listening. There is a need to control the interview and yet not engage in too much conversation ourselves.

Obviously, the interviewer learns little or nothing while talking. It is only in creating a climate that encourages the applicant to speak freely that the interviewer can gather information to help make an accurate assessment. The interviewer must strive to keep the conversation going with minimal input. The evaluation model, which is presented in Chapter 9, is designed to help minimize the problem of talking too much.

Good interviewing is not merely a matter of trading questions for answers. Instead, it requires the skill to create a purposefully directed casual conversation—one that allows the interviewer to guide the discussion from one topic to the next. Thus, the effective interviewer must learn to lead the discussion but not dominate it. Such a role requires the interviewer to be a good listener—to show genuine interest in the comments of the applicant. Of course, proficiency in listening can serve managers well in a number of other business activities such as coaching subordinates or influencing customers. It is an art that has broad application, but it is particularly essential for assessing others.

Jumping to Conclusions

When interviewers hear applicants offer information about themselves or observe some behavior pattern, there is a tendency to accept the first logical explanation of the fact or behavior rather than to recognize that many alternative conclusions are also probable. An interviewer may learn, for example, that an applicant graduated in the upper 10 percent of his or her class. The interviewer might think, "Here is a really bright individual." Now, it is quite possible the person is very bright; it is also quite possible the applicant is a person of only modest intellectual endowment who worked hard for his or her grades. The high grades may have been achieved as a result of considerable motivation and not as a function of above-average native intelligence. It may also be true that the applicant's uncle is dean of the school. A number of reasons apart from high intellect could account for the good grades.

Facts or data gleaned from an interview often lend themselves to alternative explanations. To be effective in assessing others, the interviewer must avoid making judgments too soon and must learn to evaluate data so as to select the correct interpretation of any piece of information. This book will outline a specific procedure, the hypothesis method, that will enable interviewers to reduce the tendency to draw incorrect conclusions.

Another common tendency, particularly among inexperienced interviewers, is to allow a relatively minor attribute (positive or negative) to determine a hire, not-hire decision. For example, an interviewer may be unduly influenced positively by a candidate who graduated with good grades from the same college as the interviewer. This problem is further exaggerated if the applicant also participated in many of the same extracurricular activities. Sometimes candidates are summarily rejected because they have a "weak handshake" or "didn't look me squarely in the eyes." Often other strengths and weaknesses that could lead to a different conclusion are not given sufficient weight.

In most organizations it is stated, implicitly or explicitly, that only above-average candidates are sought. Translated into operational behavior, this desire to hire "only the best" is often interpreted to mean that we don't hire people with shortcomings, although we may allow a minor one here or there. This, too, is jumping to conclusions. Each applicant represents a balance of strengths and weaknesses, so interviewers need to guard against being turned off by shortcomings in applicants. A weakness is often the reciprocal of a strength. For instance, a candidate who is highly creative and innovative may be judged by an interviewer to be too theoretical, or too "blue sky." More will be said on this topic in Chapter 6, "How to Evaluate What You Hear—A Conceptual Viewpoint."

Telegraphing the Desired Answer

Managers often ask how to avoid being fooled by experienced interview-takers. That is not easy because many applicants, particularly M.B.A.'s or college seniors, have had the opportunity to complete a course on how to take interviews; many may have participated in more interviews or be better trained than the interviewers.

How difficult or easy it is for interviewers to be fooled has to do with the practice of "telegraphing." That is, most interviewers—through their method of questioning—inadvertently suggest to the candidate the answers they would like to hear. In listening to tapes, for example, one frequently hears the question, "Did you take part in any extracurricular activities on campus?" It is obvious to the applicant, of course, that participation in extracurricular activities must be important to the interviewer. The candidate assumes it would be poorly regarded to indicate little or no involvement in such activities. Another example of telegraphing is the question, "Did you assume any leadership roles in your extracurricular activities?" Again, the interviewer fairly begs the applicant to give the appropriate answer. The interviewer thereby makes it easy for applicants to look better than they are.

Another procedure that communicates valuable cues to the applicant is to describe, early in the interview, the job requirements. To illustrate this problem, here is an example taken from an actual tape recording.

INTERVIEWER: Now one thing you should know about this job is that it requires a lot of self-starting ability. You are going to be out on your own a great deal and may see your boss only once every two weeks. And, of course, you're going to have to get your hands dirty, move crates and boxes, and there's plenty of paperwork too. There are a lot of records you need to keep. I think you should know these things before we get into this any further.

With such a description in hand, the applicant obviously understands the best way to respond when the interviewer asks questions about self-starting ability, willingness to get hands dirty, or attitude toward report writing. The applicant who really wants the job can easily supply the correct answers. Candidates who know exactly what is expected may even unintentionally engage in misrepresentation. That is, even though an applicant indicates ability and desire to do the job described, there may be other areas of work for which he or she is more skillful and from which he or she will derive greater satisfaction, but the interviewer is not likely to learn about this.

Failing to Translate Facts to On-the-Job Behavior

Of the four most commonly observed mistakes, the most serious and, at the same time, most difficult to overcome is the failure to evaluate information heard or observed during the interview. The interviewer may spend quite a bit of time with a candidate and yet at the end have little understanding about the applicant's ability to perform the job. The interviewer, of course, has gathered more facts; the difficulty is in translating these facts into meaning about on-the-job performance.

When we consider the great variety of data available from a typical employment application blank, the question must be raised as to whether or not the interviewer needs more facts. Although additional information may help round out the applicant's life story, most interviewers, who already have substantial data available from résumés, application blanks, and college transcripts, need to concentrate on trying to understand what these facts mean rather than on gathering additional historical data.

The point can be easily illustrated with the evaluation of recent M.B.A. graduates. Most students who graduate from the better graduate schools of business have had good college records, participated in extracurricular activities, and perhaps assumed some leadership roles in undergraduate school. Most of the M.B.A.'s interviewed probably will have done quite well academically in both graduate and undergraduate schools. They are, for the most part, articulate and ambitious. What distinguishes Candidate A from Candidate B? Surely there are differences even though a close examination of their records shows the two candidates to be almost equally acceptable. The differences, in large measure, center not around the facts themselves but around how and why the students achieved their accomplishments. For example, how important is it, per se, to know which subjects a candidate liked or disliked or what grades were obtained in high school?

INTERVIEWER: What subjects did you enjoy most in high school?
APPLICANT: Well, as I think about it, I really did enjoy math and the science courses best.

Gathering a series of facts such as these just for the sake of gathering them usually contributes little to an understanding of the candidate's on-the-job behavior. However, a discussion about why one had an interest in math or science could be helpful in understanding which job activities will prove rewarding.

INTERVIEWER: What would you say there was about the math or science courses that made them appealing for you?

APPLICANT: I think one thing I liked about them was that there was always a right answer. They weren't as ambiguous as the social studies or history courses in which anybody's answer was as good as anyone else's. With math, particularly, there was one correct answer, and when you got it, you knew you were right!

In this example, the applicant may be telling us something about the kind of job environment in which he or she will function best. The applicant may be communicating an uncomfortable feeling about ambiguity and a need for a job setting in which procedures or responsibilities are structured or well defined. The message may be that the applicant is likely to be uncomfortable, and perhaps ineffective, if a boss were to give an assignment by saying, "OK, it's your baby. Handle it any way you like." Of course, we cannot be sure, at this point, about our hypothesis. But if this same desire for structure or black and whiteness comes up several other times during the interview, we have begun to learn something about how the candidate will behave in a job setting.

Let us examine another example, this one focusing on the "how."

INTERVIEWER: In which subjects did you obtain your best grades?

APPLICANT: Oh, I usually got A's in history.

INTERVIEWER: What would you say there is about yourself that might account for those fine grades you received in history?

APPLICANT: Well, I guess I can attribute them to my writing ability. In the history courses we always had a lot of term papers and, you know, those blue-book exams. I suppose that writing those papers and tests just came easily to me.

In this brief dialog, the interviewer obtains some clues about what the applicant might be good at on the job. The hypothesis that needs to be checked out is that the applicant can communicate well in writing.

In essence, the interviewer needs to concentrate on the primary mission—that of trying to predict how the applicant will perform at work. To accomplish the prediction task, a method must be found to transpose data and information from a person's past to relate it to the job for which the applicant is being considered. In Chapter 7, a clearly defined procedure is described to help the interviewer convert information and facts to meaningful behavioral patterns.

Summary

There are four key problems that all interviewers encounter: Talking too much, jumping to conclusions, "telegraphing," and failing to convert obtained information to predictions about on-the-job behavior. Specific techniques can be employed to minimize the impact of these problems, so that interviewers need not be limited by them.

CHAPTER 3

Learning About Others—
What to Talk About

One of the most disconcerting aspects of interviewing, particularly for those who do not interview frequently, is to know what to talk about next. Much energy is expended in attempting to keep one step ahead of the applicant. Some interviewers follow the sequence of items as printed on an application blank; others follow some prepared guide or interview checklist. Regardless of the device used, the result is rarely the smooth-flowing discussion that most interviewers want to achieve.

One problem in deciding what to talk about is the almost limitless number of factors that have potential value to explain an individual's behavior or job performance. There are so many bits of information that seem tantalizingly interesting. To illustrate this point, a group of forty-three managers was asked to list those factors they thought were important to learn about in order to make accurate assessments of candidates for supervisory positions. They produced this list.

Analytical skills   Stability
Self-confidence   Persistence
Poise   Maturity

Quantitative skills	Ability to organize oneself
Job interests	Technical know-how
Relevant job experiences	Drive
Social perceptiveness	Ambition
Goals and objectives	Cooperativeness
Energy	Educational background
Ability to communicate	

The managers were saying, in effect, that they could predict the candidate's job success if they were able to learn about all these items. However, they also doubted that all these topics could be meaningfully explored during a typical interview. And their doubts were well taken; the subjects are numerous and complex. An interviewer might acquire a certain "feel" for some of the topics and achieve a reasonably confident understanding of others. But some qualities, such as maturity, often take years to evaluate, even if you are living with the person. To develop a significant dialog to learn about all of them is not feasible in a typical assessment interview—at least not one of less than three or four hours' duration. Every interviewer desires a well-rounded picture of the applicant, but it is not usually practical to fully discuss or evaluate the candidate on all these matters.

A second reason for the what-to-talk-about problem stems from the absence of a plan for organizing the sequence in which topics are to be discussed. The mechanics of conducting the interview should be made easy so that energy and attention can be invested in evaluating what is heard.

This chapter provides both a description of the topics the interviewer can explore and a plan for accomplishing the exploration. It should be emphasized that the interviewer does not initiate the interview with the intention of determining whether or not the applicant possesses a certain set of traits or qualities. Instead, the interviewer uses a broad topic outline that provides a springboard for conversations from which the applicant's particular strengths and limitations can emerge.

Four Basic Factors

To plan an agenda, the interviewer must first be aware of the kinds of information that are essential to know at the conclusion of the interview. A tool that can help determine which data are most critical is the statistical technique of factor analysis. This method condenses a variety of items into relatively discrete and homogeneous units. When human traits and skills are factor analyzed, psychologists are usually able to distill them into the following four basic factors that account for success at work.

1. Intellectual skills and aptitudes.
2. Motivational characteristics.
3. Personality strengths and limitations.
4. Knowledge and experience.

If the Figure 3 circle represents a total person, then it is essential to acquire information about all four factors to obtain a complete picture of the applicant. Should the interviewer fail to obtain at least some data about each of the four factors, understanding of the applicant will be incomplete and assessment will be distorted. At the conclusion of the interview, the interviewer should be able to write a descriptive paragraph about each of the factors—including the can-

FIGURE 3.   *Basic factors in each individual's makeup.*

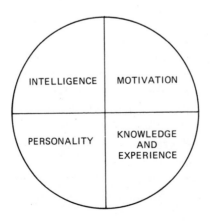

didate's basic aptitudes, thought and problem-solving processes, motivation, relationships to people and temperament, and relevance of the applicant's knowledge and work experiences to the job. In a sense, the four factors provide a gauge against which the interviewer can measure success in developing a comprehensive analysis of the candidate. It is not to be inferred, however, that each of the factors has equal weight or importance for every job. Obviously, the weighting will vary from position to position, but in no case can any one of the factors be dismissed as unimportant. In a research assignment, for instance, the intelligence and knowledge-experience factors may carry the heaviest weight. However, neither motivation nor personality factors can be ignored. If the research scientist has little ability to persuade others of the merits of his or her ideas or speculations, the researcher may receive little or no budget to accomplish his or her work. Similarly, motivation and personality factors may command more weight in the selection of successful salespersons, but the intellectual and knowledge-experience factors must also be evaluated.

Later in this chapter, techniques are described that will help ensure that the interviewer obtains information about each factor. The interviewer will be shown, through a discussion of the candidate's life history, how to accumulate information about each of the four factors. First, however, let us gain an understanding of the composition of the four factors.

Intellectual Factor

In order to understand a candidate's intellectual capabilities, intelligence must be examined from two different points of view. On the one hand, there is intellectual capacity—the innate ability to solve problems. All people are born with basic capacities that define the limits within which they can function. On the other hand, there is the question of application and effectiveness, that is, how well the individual applies and uses intellectual capacity.

There are many individuals who possess considerable capacity but who do not apply it well. For example, a person may have good basic intellectual capacity and hence the potential capability of arriving at good solutions to complex problems, but because of an impulsive or action-oriented nature, his reasoning is superficial and shallow. He has good capacity, but he does not apply it effectively. Another example is a person who has excellent basic intelligence but does not conceptualize well. Such a person focuses on detail and can rarely see the forest for the trees. A third example of good capacity but poor application can be seen in the person who has fine solutions to problems or creative ideas but does not express them. Most executives know of individuals who often leave a problem-solving meeting without having expressed themselves but who, on the way back to their offices, verbalize a solution that would have been ideal. These persons often are afraid of being wrong or of being criticized; they have good ideas, but they rarely express them.

Unfortunately, there is no good way to obtain an accurate reading of a candidate's intellectual capacity during an interview. The best capacity estimates can be obtained by certain intelligence tests—tests that do not depend upon one's knowledge and for which scores are not substantially affected by one's reading ability or time pressures. These tests have no time limits and provide a measure of one's ability to solve increasingly complex problems.[1] For example, the test items may be like the ones below.

Because the test items are graded in difficulty, that is, each one is slightly more difficult than the preceding one, eventually each applicant reaches items for which he or she cannot conceptualize correct solutions despite having all the

Complete the series by adding the next number or letter.

(a) 2   4   6   8   10   ?

(b) a   b   x   c   d   x   e   f   x   ?

(c) 3   7   23   95   ?

(d) a   c   c   b   e   a   ?

[1] An example of such an instrument is the *Analytical Judgment Test*, published by Psychological Publications Company, Box 216, Kennebunkport, Maine 04046.

time that is desired. There is no way, however, that similar estimates can be accomplished through interviewing.

When an estimate of the applicant's intellectual capacity is deemed necessary (it should be of great concern if potential for advancement is a consideration in the hire, not-hire decision), then capacity must be measured by tests or must be inferred from past school or work achievements. Reasonably accurate inferences about capacity often can be made if the applicant has an extensive work history. In such cases, the interviewer can obtain some estimate of capacity by evaluating the complexity of the tasks the applicant has successfully completed. Similarly, when inferring capacity from schoolwork, the assumption can reasonably be made that adequate capacity exists if the applicant achieved upper-third grades from one of the better colleges or universities. In studies completed by psychologists in a research project, it was found that the basic capacity of seventy-six top executives for several *Fortune* 500 firms was somewhat (ten percentile points) above average when compared with scores on the same test from a cross section of recent college graduates. Of course, these top executives are very superior in capacity when compared with a general cross section of male adults. In any event, in order to get to the top in large U.S. corporations, executives usually need above-average, but not extremely high, capacities when compared with college graduates.

Apparently, an executive's ability to advance, given the capacity level defined here, depends on other qualities than sheer brainpower. If the applicant is an excellent student at one of the better colleges, his intellectual capacity is likely to be sufficient for potential growth into most key positions, all other factors being satisfactory. The question that needs to be answered is, How effectively can the candidate use the capacity he or she has?

As the interview proceeds, the interviewer should be noting such points as these about the applicant's use of his capacity: How does he organize his thoughts? Logically? Scattered? How effectively does he communicate? How does he think—is he reflective or impulsive? Is his thinking penetrating or shallow? Can he be concise and to the point or does he go off on tangents? Can he think under pressure? What kinds of intellectual skills have been developed? What kinds of natural intellectual aptitudes does the candidate possess?

Motivation Factor

The motivation factor can be evaluated by learning what a person likes to do or finds satisfaction in doing. Some writers refer to motivation as the "will do" factor, while intelligence, knowledge, and personality represent the "can do" factors. In learning about a candidate's motivation, it is helpful to explore three basic areas: the applicant's interests, aspirations, and energy level.

Interests. One of the easiest ways to learn about an individual's motivation is to inquire about likes and dislikes. Each time interviewees tell you they have done something, you can easily inquire what was liked or disliked about the activity. However, when inquiring about interests, it is not enough to ask only about reactions. It is usually necessary to take a "second cut" at the question; that is, the interviewer must follow up the first question with a second inquiry about the reason for the applicant's preference. The point in asking about the "why" of an interest can be illustrated by examining the following interview segment.

INTERVIEWER: Which of those three summer jobs would you say you enjoyed the most?
APPLICANT: The drafting job.

At this point, what does the interviewer really know? Hearing that the applicant enjoyed the drafting work tells almost nothing about the applicant's motivational pattern. It is almost always essential, therefore, to follow the fact-seeking question with a second, motivation-seeking question.

INTERVIEWER: What was it about the drafting job that made it appealing for you?
APPLICANT: I think what I liked about that job is that they left me pretty much on my own and weren't always looking over my shoulder. I had my drawings to do, but as long as I got them done on schedule, how and when I did them was left up to me.

From the applicant's explanation, we see immediately that it wasn't so much the nature of the work that he enjoyed, but rather the freedom or independence to work on his own. In the example cited, the follow-up question helped the interviewer avoid a mistaken interpretation that might have been inferred from the first response, namely, that the drafting work itself was the main source of satisfaction.

It should also be recognized that the interviewer is not likely to learn whether or not a candidate likes a given job by asking directly how the candidate feels about doing that kind of work. For example, it would be inappropriate to ask, "Now that you have had a chance to learn something about the work here, do you think you would enjoy being a technical service representative with us?" [2]

The question invites the applicant to deceive the interviewer. If the candidate really wants the job, the correct answer is obvious. Of course, there are some applicants who will be open and frank concerning their feelings about the job in question. However, it is difficult to distinguish between those who indicate they would like the job because it is the right thing to say and those who indicate a positive preference because they truly like the kind of work being offered.

Thus, the prudent strategy is to inquire frequently throughout the interview about the candidate's likes and dislikes in a wide range of activities, many of which may be quite unrelated to the job. In this way, a less distorted picture of the applicant's true activity preference is likely to emerge. For instance, suppose the interviewer asked the candidate what he or she enjoyed least about summer jobs held while attending college. The applicant usually will not relate the question to the job to be filled and, consequently, will speak quite honestly. It is in this manner, by asking many "like" and "dislike" questions, that the interviewer learns about the applicant's true feelings and acquires an accurate picture of the candidate's motivational pattern.

Aspirations. Discussion of the person's objectives or goals

---

[2] This kind of question can be used near the end of the interview. At that time, it is appropriate to inquire what there is about the job that might be appealing and not appealing.

is another way of obtaining information about an individual's motivation. In particular, it can provide clues as to what one seeks from one's work efforts, one's value system, and one's perception of the world. However, these are matters about which the applicant can easily deceive the interviewer. Deception is particularly likely when interviewing college seniors or M.B.A.'s. Almost all have been counseled by placement directors as to the importance of having meaningful goals and objectives. Even the untrained have the sophistication to know it is not desirable to tell a potential employer that one has no particular targets or goals. Most applicants will be able to delineate in rather careful detail their goals and objectives. However, the mere fact that they describe them in a way that seems to suggest they have a clear career path in mind is no guarantee that they are actually committed to such objectives. A discussion about how to manage the conversation about goals and objectives appears later in this chapter.

The interviewer needs to test the validity of a polished answer by asking the candidate why he or she has picked a particular career path or why one's particular goals are most ideal. The individual who has thought through goals and objectives and has valid reasons for selecting them usually can handle this question quite effectively; those who are simply attempting to impress the interviewer usually find it difficult to express sound reasons for their decisions, and their thinking will appear shallow and superficial. Again, the motivational input we are seeking comes not so much from the specific goals or objectives mentioned but from the reasons the applicant cites for selecting the goals.

Energy level. While analysis of an individual's interests and goals provides some understanding of the kinds of activities that will motivate the candidate, there is also a second question to be asked, namely, how far down the road will this motivation take the applicant? In other words, direction is one thing, but strength and force in that direction is another. The amount of energy an individual can apply to work activities is a significant variable in job success. Thus, energy level is an important component of the motivational factor.

Energy refers to the physical and biological potential that

an individual possesses. A high energy level implies the ability to work long hours without tiring and the ability to get by with relatively little sleep and yet show considerable zest and vitality. This physical energy potential is usually ascertained by inquiring about the activity level of candidates. A person with a high energy level usually seems to keep going effectively for long hours in fairly demanding activities. One way to obtain a rough assessment of a person's energy level is to ask the candidate to describe a typical Tuesday in his or her life. A male executive with a high energy level might respond as follows:

APPLICANT: Well, I'm usually up pretty early. I like to get into the office before the staff and get most of the paperwork out of the way, so I'm up at 6 A.M. and usually on the 7:30 train. And I'm at the office usually till about 5:30 or 6 P.M. I get home around 7 o'clock, have dinner, let's see now, Tuesday is Board of Education night. I'm on the board and usually get out to the meeting at 8 and try to get home by 11 or so. Most nights I try to catch the 11 o'clock news. By then, the house has quieted down and I find it's a good time to go over papers I've brought from the office—I usually try to get to bed around 12:15 or so.

Persons with high energy typically will show a fair amount of zest and vitality in the employment interview. It should be recognized, of course, that energy, as with most human traits, distributes itself on a normal curve. To be an acceptable candidate, not everyone need be a bundle of energy. It is important, however, that the interviewer be alert to individuals who appear to have relatively low energy levels—particularly if growth potential is of importance or if the job involves extraordinary physical demands, such as extensive travel, long work hours, and so forth.

Personality Factor

The personality factor refers to three different but highly interrelated elements: psychological adjustment, interpersonal relationships, and temperament. To obtain data for these elements, the focus should be on acquiring information about two basic abilities—the applicant's skill in interpersonal relationships and in coping with work demands.

Adjustment. This element has to do with the applicant's general state of mental health. Obviously, if the interviewer is not trained in psychology or psychiatry, accurate diagnosis of mental or emotional condition is unrealistic. However, the interviewer can and should be alert to the presence of self-defeating behavior patterns. A blatant example would be an applicant who shows evidence of being a problem drinker. More subtle self-defeating adjustment patterns might be seen in an applicant who is forceful and aggressive to the point of being so overbearing that others avoid contact with the individual. Or, a candidate may have learned to adjust to stresses in his or her environment by retreating from or avoiding problems or difficulties, rather than confronting them.

Destructive or self-defeating psychological adjustments are not encountered in a large proportion of applicants. In those situations in which evidence indicates consistent patterns of problem behavior, the impact of such behavior should be judged in relationship to all the other strengths and limitations of the applicant.

Interpersonal relationships. Information about interpersonal relationships is obtained from two sources: observed behavior during the interview, that is, how the applicant interacts with the interviewer, and evidence of how the candidate interacted with others in the past.

Let's look first at the input from the applicant's ongoing behavior vis-à-vis the interviewer during the interview. Here is a source of information that can be obtained in no other way—how the applicant relates to you as a person, that is, the chemistry that exists between the two of you. This information is critical if the applicant is going to work directly for you. Thus, as interviewers conduct the session, they should note their feelings about the candidate as well as the applicant's apparent reactions o the interview discussion. Is the applicant shy? Confident? Aggressive? Withdrawn? Forceful? Persuasive? Bitter? Arrogant? Open? Outgoing? Passive? Dependent?

What is he or she like? If the interview is conducted

properly, the interviewer should have ample opportunity to begin developing a picture of how this person typically behaves when he is attempting to create a positive impression and how comfortable and compatible the applicant might be to work with on the job.

Many books about interviewing point out that the interviewer needs to guard against judgments that are distorted by biases and prejudices. Such caution is well taken. But, at the same time, no magic switch exists that the interviewer can turn on to automatically permit him or her to become objective. Biases are always with us. One effective way to cope with prejudices is to recognize their presence and try to understand how they are affecting the employment decision.

Once in a while, an interviewer may see a candidate about whom he has vague, but negative, feelings. The interviewer, if pressed to explain why he or she does not like the candidate, would probably find it difficult to give a logical explanation. The interviewer is often inclined to attribute negative impressions to some bias or prejudice. We do this because there is a psychological need to provide a reason for our feelings; if none is apparent, we make one up. The interviewer who encounters an applicant he or she does not like but who cannot explain those feelings, should not dismiss the attitude as a bias but should heed vague I-can't-put-my-finger-on-it feelings. Many subtle and nonverbal clues are transmitted in face-to-face encounters. If the candidate creates a negative impression upon the interviewer, something is definitely causing it.

Usually, the negative feelings of the interviewer result from the applicant's attitude. The applicant may have been too aggressive, snobbish, pushy, or arrogant. It may be that the applicant talked down to the interviewer. It is not so much what the applicant said, but more how it was said, and the subtlety of this often escapes us.

Let me cite an extreme example of what can happen if interviewers do not pursue their feelings about an applicant. A large machine-tool company had hired a plant manager and now the president and his two vice-presidents bemoaned that they had to fire him after only one week of employment. During the discussion, one of the vice-presidents said, "You know, when I was interviewing that man, I had a funny feeling about him. I couldn't put my finger on it, but something just didn't seem right." The other vice-president made a similar comment. The president, too, said, "You know, I had the same kind of feeling." They had just learned that the person they had hired had not graduated from the college he had indicated and he had falsified much of his employment record. In the interviews, he appeared to be a polished, articulate individual who knew the industry sufficiently well to make a favorable impression on the president, two vice-presidents, and the company's personnel director. It was only through a somewhat delayed routine credit check that the discrepancies were uncovered.

Here was a case in which three individuals all had the vague feeling that something was wrong but dismissed it. It is important that the interviewer consider how the candidate impresses him as a person and try to understand how and why this impression is occurring.

The second element in understanding an applicant's interpersonal skills relates to how the candidate interacts with others. Information can be acquired by reviewing the candidate's life history, with emphasis on learning how the candidate dealt with various interpersonal confrontations. Throughout the interview, the interviewer should obtain a description of how each personal interaction was handled. For instance, if a female applicant indicates that she earned all her spending money at college by selling *Time* subscriptions on campus, the interviewer might ask, "What would you say you did, in talking with the students, that led to your success in selling the magazines?" Or the interviewer might pose this question, "Suppose you ran into a student who was particularly negative to your sales presentation and really gave you a hard time. How did you typically manage a situation like that?"

Here's one more example:

INTERVIEWER: You mentioned that you left your last job because of limited opportunity for advancement. I was wondering, did you talk with your boss about possibilities for growth in the firm?

APPLICANT: Oh, yes, several times.

INTERVIEWER: Well, when you went to discuss promotion possibilities with your boss, tell me what you said and how you approached it.

Each time the applicant mentions an interaction with others, try to get a description of the behavior pattern followed. This information, when added to the observed hypotheses made about the applicant's behavior during the interview, should enable the interviewer to evolve the confirmed hypotheses about interpersonal relationships and to write a meaningful paragraph or two about how the candidate relates to others in a wide range of situations.

Temperament. The third element that helps to explain the personality factor is the individual's approach to work situations, namely, the applicant's temperament. Is the applicant compulsive? Rigid? Energetic or lethargic? Cautious? Sensitive? Impulsive? In other words, how does the candidate behave? Here again, the interviewer is not to look for certain traits or characteristics but rather let them emerge from observed behavior and from hypotheses developed from self-appraisal questions about the applicant's life history. Subsequent chapters describe the exact procedures for doing this.

Knowledge and Experience Factor

The fourth fundamental factor of knowledge and experience needs little explanation. Basically, to form a rounded picture of an individual, the interviewer must obtain data about the relevancy of a person's educational background and prior work experience. Is one's training and job experience appropriate and helpful to the task at hand? In what ways will the applicant's knowledge help or hinder performance? Most managers typically overestimate the specific skills required for any given task and underestimate the ability of individuals to learn what is needed to perform a new task. The interviewer must be satisfied about how capable the person is of learning the skills needed for the job in question.

In some jobs—especially those involving technology—it is

obvious that the depth and extent of the applicant's capabilities must be carefully explored. Even in such cases, however, if the interviewers are experienced in the particular field, it usually is not difficult to develop a line of questioning that will reveal strengths and weaknesses in knowledge. The depth of know-how can often be revealed by asking the candidate to discuss how and why key projects were completed in past assignments. It is frequently helpful to ask applicants to explain their perceptions of the current state of the art in their respective field.

In attempting to evaluate a candidate's technical competence, some interviewers like to use short verbal tests. They pose a hypothetical problem situation and then ask the applicants what solutions they favor.

There is nothing wrong with the use of such tests, as long as conclusions are not drawn from them on the basis of whether or not the correct answer is given. The validity of a one- or two-item test to accurately predict success is extremely low. Reliability is largely a matter of the number of test items. If the interviewer asked thirty or forty "how-would-you-solve" kind of questions, much more confidence could be placed on the meaning of the applicant's responses than if only one or two such problems were presented.

On the other hand, it is valid and appropriate for the interviewer to ask how the applicant would solve specific technical problems if the interviewer uses the test question as a basis for observing how the candidate handles himself or herself, the methods used to solve the problem, the sophistication of knowledge displayed, and so on, instead of whether or not the answer is correct. In other words, if the test question is not used as a pass–fail sort of quiz, but rather as a means to observe application of knowledge, then its use can be helpful.

Obtaining Data on the Four Factors

We have said thus far that in order to do a competent and thorough assessment of any job candidate, it is necessary to obtain some information about each of the four factors described here. Obviously, it is impossible to know everything about a person's intellectual makeup, motivation, personality, and knowledge and experience, but if data about any one of those factors are omitted from the assessment, a large portion of what figures in job success will not be accounted for, and the predictions of the interviewer will be seriously handicapped.

Chapter 9 will provide a model or procedure for conducting the interview to help ensure that all four factors are explored. At this point, it may be helpful for the interviewer to institute an interview plan. This means that the interviewer sets up a series of significant topics to be discussed in the interview, and that the interviewer proceeds in every interview to follow the same organizational format, using the same topic sequence in each interview. If one thinks about it, there are a limited number of topics that can be legitimately covered in the interview. Here are the major life areas that the interviewer is likely to touch on:

1. High school.
2. College and/or specialized training.
3. Military experiences.
4. Work experiences—full time.
5. Work experiences—summer and part time.
6. Attitude toward job, company, or industry.
7. Career goals and/or ambitions.
8. Candidate's own assessment of strengths and limitations.
9. Present activities and interests.

Obviously, if the candidate did not attend college or was not in the service, those areas would be omitted from the interview plan. The plan should not necessarily follow the order indicated here. In evolving your interview plan, it is probably best to start off with topic areas that are relatively easy for the applicant to talk about. For example, if most of the candidates to be interviewed are young college graduates, one might start off talking about education and their college experiences. On the other hand, if the interviewer typically interviews mature senior executives, the plan might begin by asking the applicants to review their work experiences.

The interviewer may also want to include, early in the interview plan but not necessarily as the first topic, parts of the person's life that are more important as opposed to the less critical. For example, with an experienced executive, it may be better to begin the interview with work experiences rather than high school or present activities. Also, it is helpful to put the more threatening areas such as self-assessment of strengths and limitations near the end of the interview. Other than that, there is no magic to the sequence followed. The main point is to establish a plan and to follow that plan in every interview. Figure 4 has two different interview plans that have proved to be effective.

There are several reasons the interview plan is suggested. It simplifies the mechanics of conducting an interview. It

FIGURE 4.   Samples of two interview plans.

Relatively Inexperienced College Grads, Middle Managers*	Experienced Senior Executives

High School
College
Work Experiences
   summer, part time
Work Experiences
   full time
Goals and Ambitions
Reactions to Job
Self-assessment
Military Experiences
Present Activities
	Work Experiences
	   full time
	College/or Studies
	Goals and Ambitions
	Reactions to Job
	Self-assessment
	Military Experiences
	Present Activities
	High School

*For relatively inexperienced high school graduates, the same plan can be followed, omitting the college section.

removes from the interviewer's mind the problem of what to ask next. With the plan, the interviewer always knows what will come next and, as a consequence, will have a comfortable feeling of being in control. The interviewer will always know when he or she is half way or a third of the way through the interview. So, a topic sequence plan makes the conduct of the interview relatively easy. It also makes possible a smooth transition from one area to the next.

A second and perhaps more important reason for having an interview plan is to ensure that the interviewer cuts through a broad cross section of the individual's life. As we shall learn when we talk about evaluating data, it is important to develop hypotheses for all four factors. If the interviewer restricts questions essentially to education or job experiences, the profile will emphasize those factors and may not yield enough data about motivation and personality.

Life Areas to Explore

High School

It is important to note that if it has been many years since the candidate attended high school, the interviewer should not be concerned with specific facts about what the applicant did or did not do. After all, if high school was attended twenty years earlier in the applicant's life, the relevancy of these incidents is open to question. However, even in these cases, the area is worthwhile exploring because it can provide a rich source of data and hypotheses about current behavior. The reason for this is that the applicant is interpreting the past (how and why things were done) through the perception of them today—not through the eyes and mind of a sixteen-year-old student but as a present-day adult. For example:

INTERVIEWER: You mentioned you played basketball in high school. Sometimes people learn something from playing team sports; sometimes, of course, we get nothing in particular from them. But, as you think back on that period in

your life, is there anything you think you learned from
playing on that team?
APPLICANT: Yes, I think I got something from it. I learned
that if you want to do something hard enough, you can.
INTERVIEWER: Could you elaborate on that a bit?
APPLICANT: Sure. I wasn't very tall in high school, and when I
went out for the team, the coach said that I could try out,
but he doubted I'd be big enough to make the team . . . but
I'll tell you, I was really determined, and somehow I made
it. I was just more scrappy and outran the bigger guys; I
was always after the ball. I guess what I am saying is
I learned that if I set my mind on doing something,
I'm usually able to do it . . . and that's true for me even
now.

TOPICS TO EXPLORE:

□ Best subjects; subjects done less well.
    What made them easy? Difficult?
□ Subjects liked the most; liked the least.
    Why was that subject so appealing?
    Not appealing?
□ Extracurricular activities.
    What was learned from them?
□ Early interests and ambitions (even if they now sound
    silly).
    What made these appealing?

College and Other Studies

As is true for the high school area, exploration of college
experiences provides good opportunity to learn about intellectual skills and aptitudes, motivational patterns (by asking
about likes and dislikes of subjects and school activities), and
personality makeup such as adaptability, perseverance, social
adeptness, and so forth.

If several schools were attended, it is recommended that
each school be discussed in some depth as a relatively separate issue.

- ☐ Same topics as high school.
- ☐ Reason for selection of major.
- ☐ Reasons for selecting school.
- ☐ Reasons for changes in curriculum (if any).
    What were the factors that led to your decision to change?
- ☐ Extent education will aid work.
    In what ways do you see your educational background helping you succeed in this job?

Military Experience

Prolonged or detailed discussion of a candidate's military career usually is not productive for predicting on-the-job behavior. However, from time to time the interviewer can learn about skills acquired, attitudes (particularly about highly structured environments), and personality characteristics such as adaptability.

Topics to Explore:

- ☐ Assignments and duties.
- ☐ Explanation for advancement or lack of it.
- ☐ What was learned from military experiences?
- ☐ What was hoped to be gained? (if voluntary)

Work Experiences

It is usually desirable to cover work experiences in chronological order. This procedure enables the interviewer to look for gaps in the employment record and to understand the rationale behind the applicant's job changes. The interviewer should always be certain to inquire why the applicant made each job change and what was seen in the new assignment that made it more desirable than the prior one.

It is also helpful to ask for salary information as each job is discussed. More specifically, ask the applicant to state both starting and ending salaries. If salary information is requested for the first few jobs that applicants have had, they will usually pick up the train of thought and provide salary data about subsequent jobs without the interviewer having to ask for it. Salary history is also relatively easy to confirm, thereby providing a good means of checking on the credibility of the applicant's statements about job responsibilities.

Summer or part-time employment should be considered as a separate area for exploration, unless the applicant voluntarily describes such employment along with the description of full-time jobs. The same kinds of topics can be explored for full-time and part-time work experiences.

TOPICS TO EXPLORE:

- Things done best; done less well.
  What skills did you bring to bear that made it possible? What about your personal makeup might have accounted for your success?
- Job activities liked best; disliked.
  What was there about them that was appealing?
- Major accomplishment on each job.
  How were you able to do it? What did you have going for you that made it possible?
- Most difficult problems encountered.
  How did you solve them? What made them difficult?
- How people relationships were handled.
  What did you do that made it work out? If you could do it over, how would you handle it differently?
- Reasons for changing jobs.

Attitudes Toward Job and Company

In this section of the interview plan, the interviewer solicits the applicant's attitudes and feelings about the company, the job, or the industry for which he or she is applying.

TOPICS TO EXPLORE:

- Interests about job.
  What is it about this job that might be appealing to you? What do you see in this assignment that was not available to you in your prior assignment? I realize that you are not yet in this job and therefore cannot answer this question very accurately, but what things

do you think you'll be doing that might be somewhat less than satisfying for you? No job is altogether perfect, but from what you may know at this point, what is the least satisfactory aspect of this job?

□ Reactions to company or organization.

Is there anything about our organization that might raise a question in your mind as to how ideal this is for you as a place to work?

□ Reactions to the industry.

How do you feel about our industry (or line of business)?

□ Job perceptions.

What do you feel you might have to know more about before you could really step in and do this assignment justice?

Aspirations and Goals

Exploration of the applicant's ambitions is an important part of the interview because it aids in establishing additional data and hypotheses about motivation. It provides the interviewer with information about activities in which the applicant expects to find satisfaction as well as those that the applicant wants to avoid. It also helps to obtain further understanding of the applicant's drive and ambitions for the future.

The classic approach to discussing goals is to ask, "Where would you like to be five years from now?" However, anyone who has done a fair amount of interviewing knows that of all the questions one could ask this question yields answers that can be quite deceiving; almost all reasonably sophisticated applicants will have a prepared or canned answer. Applicants often state their response with a great sense of conviction, even though they may be uncertain as to goals or career direction. In effect, they simply state a logical answer in order to appear reasonable to the interviewer.

Interviewers need to be careful not to be unduly impressed by applicants who seem to know where they want to go, or unimpressed by the applicant who seems somewhat confused or uncertain as to vocational or career goals. Instead, the interviewer should try to understand the rationale or underlying reasons why the applicant indicates the goals mentioned. In this way, meaningful data can be obtained about the applicant's motivation and interests.

In brief, then, the question about goals and ambitions is asked not so much for the direct response that is given by the applicant but because the response provides a jumping off point for the interviewer to explore further how or why the goals were selected. Let's consider an example. Here's a dialog situation between an interviewer and an applicant who seems, at the outset, sure and confident about his goals. However, as will be apparent by the end of the example, the applicant is really uncertain as to his ambitions.

INTERVIEWER: As you look down the road ahead, where would you like to see yourself five years from now?

APPLICANT: Well, I feel fairly confident about what I want to do. I want to move up the sales ladder, and my expectation is that within a year I'll be moving into some first-level supervisory position. Beyond that, it's hard to put an exact timetable on it, but I would think I could be a district sales manager within three to four years. Then, I would hope to move right on up to become a regional manager in maybe five to six years.

INTERVIEWER: Well, that certainly sounds as though you've made up your mind where you want to go and how rapidly you want to move. Tell me, what makes you feel so certain that this is the best career path for you?

APPLICANT: That's a good question. [Pauses] As a matter of fact, I have been looking at other opportunities in market research. I think the challenges in the research area could be very appealing. I guess what I'm saying here is that my mind isn't really so closed. I would want to see what market research might have to offer in comparison to the sales jobs.

INTERVIEWER: Well, suppose you tell me a little about what you see market research work offering you that you may not find in sales work?

APPLICANT: That's a real tough one. I guess I'm really going to have to first dig a little deeper into the sales jobs in order to see what there is about them that will be the most satisfying for me. Then perhaps I'll be able to compare better.

People who have thought out their career plans carefully and have a true commitment to them usually have a reasoned approach for stating their goals and objectives and can verbalize these thoughts in a clear, believable way. On the other hand, those who define some goals according to what they believe is the right thing to say usually are unable to convincingly explain why they made the choices they have indicated. If questioned, some will tell you that they are still uncertain as to what they want to do. In any event, the important point here is that one should not take at face value a person's description of goals and objectives. Instead, inquiries must be made as to how the choice was reached. Hypotheses about the applicant's directional motivation and drive are then formed on the basis of reasons provided by the applicant.

At times, applicants will seem to be confused about which career paths they wish to follow, but as the interviewer explores further the motivational pattern is not at all ambiguous. This is reflected in the following dialog.

INTERVIEWER: As you look ahead, where do you see yourself going from here?

APPLICANT: Well, I guess I'm still a bit on the fence. I think I want to be in the accounting field, but I don't know whether I really want to go into auditing work with one of the large public accounting firms or take a position in finance, like the one you are offering me here.

INTERVIEWER: I can see that you feel there might be good opportunities in both fields. Tell me a little bit about your thinking on the subject. What is making it difficult for you to decide at this point?

APPLICANT: Well, I certainly want to move ahead in the business world. And it seems to me that the experience and advancement I would get in an operating company like yours are essential ingredients for getting into management. But I keep thinking that maybe the professional training I would get in an accounting firm would provide a stronger base to start out from.

INTERVIEWER: The thing that is really creating a dilemma for you is how much weight to put on the kind of training you'll get in public accounting. You're not in a quandary about what kind of work you would prefer.

APPLICANT: That's right. If I thought I'd get the same kind of training here in a business firm, then I guess my dilemma would really be resolved.

As the example demonstrates, once understanding is reached as to why the individual is confused about career goals, seemingly confused motivation becomes understandable. In fact, the interviewer will often find that no basic goal conflict exists. The interviewer, too, should be aware that many times an applicant cannot decide between career A and career B because the candidate does not have adequate knowledge of what the jobs entail. However, the interviewer should know, by virtue of an extensive review of the applicant's likes and dislikes, what kind of work will be most appealing to the candidate, even if the applicant is uncertain.

TOPICS TO EXPLORE:

- □ Short-term goals.
- □ Long-term career objectives.
    What do you feel you need before you'll be able to· qualify for such a position?
- □ Jobs or activities to be avoided in future jobs.
    Why?
- □ Salary goals or targets.
- □ Past experiences that led to present career objectives.
- □ Attitudes about travel.
    On the average, how many nights away from home per week would you consider to be excessive?
- □ Attitudes about relocating.

Self-Assessment of Candidate's Strengths and Limitations

Because this topic can be a bit threatening, the self-assessment query should be introduced near the end of the interview. Basically the interviewer asks the applicant to provide an estimate of his or her strengths and limitations. The input from such a question enables the interviewer to develop many new hypotheses about the candidate and, in addition, can help confirm or reject those that were developed earlier in the interview.

Usually the self-appraisal question is best managed by discussing it in two parts—one segment to inquire about the person's strengths and the second about his or her limitations. An easy way to introduce this topic without labeling it in an obvious fashion is to make a statement such as, "We've been talking here at some length about the success you've had over the years. What would you say there is about yourself that might have accounted for the fine record you bring to us here today?"

Sometimes applicants will have a difficult time verbalizing an answer to this question. They often think in terms of skills and abilities they possess or they may even become defensive about the question. In either case, some "pump priming" is often necessary to help the individual get started talking. For example:

APPLICANT: I just don't know what to say. I guess my success really is based upon the fact that I had good experience in this industry.

INTERVIEWER: Well, sometimes it is difficult to think about ourselves in terms of traits and qualities, but do you remember when we were talking about college and how you were able to go out for sports and still make grades good enough to get on the dean's list? At that time I asked you how you were able to manage it and you said you always had a lot of energy and that you could get along with relatively little sleep—that you were just a very vital person. Well, that might be a good quality or trait that accounted for some of your success over the years. Can you think of any other traits or abilities you have that could explain your success?

If the interviewer receives only one or two statements from the applicant about a trait or ability, the candidate should be encouraged to continue. This can be done by asking, "Is there anything else you can think of?" Almost invariably, if applicants are prompted in this way, they will offer additional thoughts. It is quite important, too, to generate a fair number of positive responses about strengths, because elaboration of them makes it easier for the applicant to answer subsequent questions about limitations.

The second part of the self-assessment area centers around shortcomings. Of course, this is a more difficult question for the applicant to respond to, but the extent of the response depends in large measure on how the question is put to the applicant. One approach is to say, "We've been talking here about all the good qualities and abilities you have; now how about the other side of the coin? What would you say there is about yourself you think could be improved upon or strengthened?"

The interviewer is likely to receive one of three typical responses to this question. First, the applicant might be open and frank and freely share his or her shortcomings. The interviewer, in such cases, can explore them in any depth desired so as to understand what the applicant is saying. A second response, however, is less helpful. The applicant may answer the question by talking about his or her knowledge or experience. Although it is helpful to understand that the applicant may feel inadequate as far as some specific knowledge or training is concerned, the stated lack of know-how is often not a significant issue in the hiring decision. Usually the interviewer has other data about the applicant's training and experience that help determine the extent of the candidate's qualifications for the job. The areas that are more important to explore in the shortcomings section are the applicant's analysis of his or her traits, personality strengths, and temperament. To direct the focus away from education and to the individual's makeup, the interviewer could ask, "Apart from knowledge—I guess we all could learn more—what would you say there is about yourself that you might wish to improve upon?"

The third typical reaction of applicants is to become defensive and beg off the question. The candidate may say, "I can't think of any serious shortcomings. Anything I've been weak in, I've worked hard to overcome."

In such cases, the interviewer should not be discouraged. It is of primary importance to encourage applicants to analyze themselves critically. In reply, the interviewer might say, "Well, I recognize that there may not be any major shortcomings in your makeup, but what might be a few of the small things that could possibly detract from 100 percent performance on your part?"

It is important not to give up too soon. This is one area in which a little pressure is acceptable. After the applicant has voiced one or two shortcomings, the interviewer should prod the individual to continue by asking, "Anything else you can think of?" It is important to continue this way, because most sophisticated applicants realize it is naive to indicate that they have no shortcomings or limitations. Thus they are likely to mention a few safe shortcomings, which often lack much depth or meaning. For example, the sophisticated applicant might indicate that she could improve her public speaking ability. Of course, almost everyone has this need, even the most polished speaker. Or another might say, "I guess I get a little impatient from time to time." Impatience has both good and bad implications: it can account for one's success and self-starting ability, and it can be seen as an undesirable personality quality. In any event, a strategy to follow when such safe responses are given is to discuss the statements made by the applicant but then go on to look for more shortcomings. Usually, after the few innocuous shortcomings are mentioned, the interviewer will uncover more significant issues about the applicant's behavior or performance.

If all efforts to encourage the applicant do not prove successful, an alternative is available. The interviewer can ask, "In what ways would you say you have grown the most over the past two to three years?" Applicants typically respond to this question by talking about a weakness. When the area of improvement is mentioned, the interviewer should draw out the candidate to learn the meaning and significance of the limitation.

Topics to Explore:

- ▫ Good qualities as seen by others (boss or teacher).
- ▫ Natural aptitude or abilities.
      Have you ever noticed any particular skill or ability
      that just came easily to you—as a natural talent?
- ▫ Qualities that make applicant a good investment.

- Areas that need improvement.

    Are there any areas you have been working on recently to help develop more job effectiveness?
- Constructive criticism heard from others.
- Ways applicant might be a risk for employer.

    Are there any things about yourself we haven't talked about that you think would help us know you better?

Leisure-Time Activities

A review of the activities that candidates enjoy in their off-hours often provides helpful input about motivation and skills. However, merely asking what a person likes to do during leisure hours is not sufficient. Usually a second-level question must be asked about the satisfactions the applicant finds in the activities mentioned. It is of little help to know that the applicant enjoys collecting stamps or manages a Little League team or putters in a garden. The real issue is what it s about this activity that makes the candidate good at it or provides him or her with personal satisfaction.

The interviewer also is cautioned to explore to what extent the applicant actually pursues leisure-time activities. It is difficult to verify whether nonwork activities are actually followed. Applicants will often reel off a string of leisure-time activities, but, upon closer examination, the interviewer finds that they engage in only one or two of them. The others were of interest earlier in life or represent peripheral interests. It is helpful, therefore, for the interviewer to explore how much time during a given month the applicant actually spends engaging in a particular activity.

TOPICS TO EXPLORE:

- Activities one likes to do in spare time.

    What about _____ do you find appealing?

    What makes you good at doing _____?
- How spare-time activities may or may not aid job performance.

Tested Questions

This chapter has suggested a variety of topics that should be discussed to ensure that sufficient data are obtained about each of the four basic factors. Also offered were a number of specific questions that can aid in achieving the same objective. These are known as tested questions; they can be defined as those that the interviewer asks in almost every interview because they have been found to produce productive and meaningful results. If the interviewer is not obtaining adequate data on one of the factors, a definite point can be made to include some tested questions that will in all probability yield data on the factor in question. To assist the interviewer in this regard, Appendix A of this book lists approximately 100 tested questions. They are cataloged by topic area, such as high school, work experience, and leisure time, and also by factor.

This is not to suggest that the interviewer conduct an entire interview with a prepared set of questions. However, a sprinkling of these tested questions throughout the interview will help ensure obtaining data on all four factors. Most individuals who have done a fair amount of interviewing will already have developed a repertoire of tested questions. Tested questions are asked at specific points during the interview, as will be explained more fully later.

Summary

In order to perform a meaningful assessment of any candidate, it is necessary to obtain data about four fundamental factors—intelligence, motivation, personality, and knowledge-experience. While it is not possible to obtain complete information about all of these elements, the absence of data on any one of the factors is a significant handicap in assessing an applicant's prospects for success at work.

The interviewer should not try to determine each of the four factors in order, but should follow an interview plan that consists of nine major topics to be explored during the interview. The plan helps the interviewer cover these nine topics in the same order in every interview. This procedure will give the interviewer a feeling of control in knowing where he or she is in the course of the interview and will also ensure wide coverage of the candidate's background. It was also suggested that tested questions be used to ensure input of ata on the four factors.

The sequence of topics to explore in the interview plan depends upon the category of candidates being interviewed. It is recommended the interviewer develop a plan that is appropriate to the general age and experience level of the individual being interviewed.

CHAPTER 4

Learning About Others— Climate

There are many theories about interviewing. Everyone has heard of the executive who, after a few preliminary remarks, picks a crayon off his desk, thrusts it in the applicant's face, and says, "Go ahead, sell me this crayon. Quick, sell it to me!" Another manager may offer cigarettes in a room in which there are no ashtrays, or three or four executives may simultaneously give an applicant the third degree.

All these techniques fall under the category of stress interview. They put applicants under duress to see how well they handle themselves or are able to cope with pressure. The question is whether or not such techniques help the executive learn much about the applicant. There is little evidence to suggest that this approach to interviewing is productive. In fact, most studies show, even when one is attempting simply to measure the candidate's skill in coping with stress or pressure, that the interview judgment of this ability usually bears little relationship to actual job performance. In other words, the use of situational tests has been singularly unsuccessful in predicting future job behavior. The exception is the use of trial experiences to determine a specific technical skill. For example, actual job conditions can be duplicated by setting up a turret lathe on which the candidate demonstrates proficiency.

One of the difficulties in using situational interviews is that it is almost impossible to duplicate a truly lifelike situation. For example, if the applicant is a candidate for a sales representative position, the interviewer can never duplicate the same stresses that the salesperson will experience in the field. Such replication is difficult because an individual's reaction to stress and pressure is a function of many different elements—the exact situation, the salesperson's self-confidence level, personality traits, temperament, and skills and abilities. In other words, as the salesperson works on the job, the factors in the equation change. Experience with other buyers, for example, will affect one's confidence level and skill in coping with tough buyers. Thus behavior during such an interview may not give an accurate impression of how the applicant will behave on the job.

Elaborate studies about the effectiveness of situational tests were conducted by the Office of Strategic Services during World War II. The findings indicated that such methods do not lend themselves well to use by amateur assessors. And, even though assessment centers have recently been demonstrated to be reasonably effective in predicting job success, the kind of job simulations to which the candidates are exposed (in-baskets, leaderless group discussions, and so forth) are far more elaborate than the kind of interview simulations referred to here.

A second reason situational tests, such as the stress interview, are not recommended is that this interview approach tends to make it more difficult to explore other facets of the candidate's makeup apart from ability to cope with stress or pressure. Indeed, use of such interviews even makes it difficult to learn about the positive aspects of the applicant's life history.

The moment stress and pressure are applied, the applicant becomes more defensive, more guarded, and less open. To make an effective assessment, the interviewer cannot just measure reaction to pressure, or social skills, or whatever. There is a need to look at the person as a totality in order to accurately evaluate future performance. Thus the approach recommended is one that creates a climate in which the candidate feels comfortable and where threat is kept to a minimal level.

Low-Threat Climate

It is quite apparent that getting applicants to talk about themselves during interviews is really not enough. To make an accurate assessment, the interviewer needs to hear about the bad as well as the good. This means applicants must be encouraged to talk about things they would prefer not to talk about. Thus the problem is to create a situation or climate in which applicants will share some of the negative elements in their past.

To obtain a better understanding of the conditions that lend themselves to openness and frankness, think of the kind of climate that would have to exist before you would be willing to reveal things about yourself that would not make you feel defensive. Most likely, words such as *sincere, confidential, friendly, relaxed,* and *understanding* will come to your mind. If all the conditions described by these words are combined, the situation created could be characterized as being relatively free of threat. It is only the threat of embarrassment, of not being thought well of, or of not being highly regarded that keeps one from revealing negatives about oneself.

Of course, no interview can be threat free. The mere fact that the discussion is an employment interview results in a certain amount of threat—even if the interview is only for practice or to visit a particular city on a recruiting trip. The candidate's ego demands that he make a good impression on the interviewer even in such a case.

How to Keep Threat Low

There are a number of activities in which the interviewer can engage in order to keep the threat level relatively low during the interview. Conceptually speaking, individuals are less threatened if they feel confident of themselves in the interview situation; that is, the extent to which applicants feel they are doing well and making favorable impressions on the interviewer is the extent to which they are likely to be open and willing to share shortcomings with the interviewer. It is much the same as with a person who is highly self-confident. The strong, confident individual normally is not afraid to point out shortcomings to others; those who are insecure or uncertain of themselves find it difficult to admit their inadequacies to others or even to themselves.

Let us examine now some ways in which this might be accomplished.

Living Room Atmosphere

There are simple social actions that the interviewer can take to make the interview situation less formal, more comfortable, and more relaxed. These include such things as speaking to the applicant on a first-name basis, offering him coffee or cigarettes, or even having a less formal sitting arrangement, such as sitting side by side rather than using a desk. Generally, gestures that feel comfortable and natural for the interviewer tend to make the climate favorable for interviewing.

Interviewers should be cautioned, however, not to play a role. Many texts about interviewing suggest that the interviewer adopt the posture of a "nice guy." The theory is that, if applicants think that the interviewer is a person who is pleasant and easygoing, they will feel more comfortable and reveal more of themselves. However, the applicant is also judging the interviewer as a potential boss. Playing a role, therefore, presents the danger that the interviewer may not come across in a sincere manner and may be seen as a bit of a phony. Thus the applicant may decide the interviewer is not the kind of manager for whom he or she would like to work.

For this reason, it is better to be yourself and to act in a natural, normal manner. Extra attention, however, should be given to the social amenities to make the situation less formal and more cordial and relaxed.

Privacy

There is no question but that people are likely to be more open if they feel their remarks are not being shared with others and there is a sense of confidentiality to the discussion. However, privacy is more than four walls; it is also related to interruptions. Whenever an interruption occurs during the interview, whether it is a telephone call or a secretary coming into the office, it provides opportunity for applicants to think about what they have been saying. It is this review of the prior stages of the interview that can create problems for the interviewer. If the interviewer is distracted for any extended period of time, the following thoughts, for example, may go through an applicant's mind: "I probably shouldn't have said so much about the fact that I was fired from the summer job in the road department. I bet this guy feels that I don't get along too well with others. I had better be sure to make the point that I'm cooperative and that I rarely have problems with people." Or the applicant might think, "This interviewer seemed quite concerned about the extracurricular activities I had in high school. They must be important to him—I'd better get a few more lined up for college because I'm sure he's going to ask about them."

It may be far better to interview in a crowded dining room and not be interrupted than to talk in a private office where interruptions occur during the discussion. If it is impossible to discontinue phone calls, it might be better to interview in a waiting room or conference room or over coffee in the cafeteria.

Small Talk

Many interviewers think that a good way to put the applicant at ease at the beginning of the interview is to engage in small talk. The idea of getting the applicant talking early in the interview is an excellent one. Whether or not small talk produces the desired climate depends a great deal upon how it is used. Not all small talk reduces tension. For example, suppose your boss calls you into his office and says, "Have a seat. Say, how are the kids?" Does his attempt at small talk put you at ease?

Getting the applicant to talk at the beginning of the interview is desirable for two reasons. First, once one has heard one's own voice in an unfamiliar setting, there is an inclination to continue verbalizing and participating in the discussion. Second, talking tends to reduce tension. Verbalizing usually helps individuals to discharge nervous energy. Thus the applicant is inclined to be less keyed up and to talk in a more spontaneous manner.

For small talk to be effective, it should not be perceived as obvious small talk. For instance, to raise questions about the weather or last week's football game or similar topics that are obviously polite chitchat may actually increase tension. The applicant is waiting until the interviewer says, "Now to start with the interview. . . ."

While there may be some value in observing how skillfully the applicant converses in a casual, small-talk way, the amount of time consumed for such knowledge probably is disproportionate to the gain. Subsequent chapters will point out other opportunities for observing the candidate's skill in coping with relatively nonstructured social situations.

The most helpful small talk stems from topics that arise naturally and spontaneously. Small talk that is obviously related to the interview situation is also good. The interviewer might, for example, ask about possible difficulties the applicant encountered in finding a parking space; or if this interview happens to be one of several, inquiry could be made about how the interviews are coming along, or how the applicant feels at this point after completing several interviews.

If the interviewer finds any strain in trying to generate small talk, it is best to avoid it altogether. After polite greetings, there is no reason not to launch right into the interview, starting off with the first area in the interviewer's scheduled interview plan. This topic should be one that is relatively easy for the applicant to talk about. If, for example, the applicant was recruited on campus and has come to the home office for a second interview, the interviewer might start out by asking about the candidate's college career. This topic is easy for the student to discuss, and it places no particular burden on the interviewer.

Structure

Anything that can be done to reduce, for the applicant, the number of unknowns about the interview process will also help reduce tension. One of the easiest things to do is to tell the applicant something about yourself. Don't give a long job history, of course, but simply mention your position in the company and briefly describe what you do. This information will help the applicant understand how much technical detail to provide about one's background and whether or not technical jargon would be understood.

It is also desirable to explain what will happen during the interview process. You can mention who else the applicant will be talking with, how long the other interviews will be (if others are already scheduled), what will happen about lunch, and when during the interview the applicant will have an opportunity to inquire about the organization.

It is also helpful to indicate that the interview will be a two-way street, that while the applicant will be expected to discuss himself or herself fully and openly, an opportunity will also be provided to learn about the organization.

Here is a statement that has worked well for me:

INTERVIEWER: Obviously you're here today to learn about job opportunities with us, just as we need to become acquainted with you. So, let's plan on dividing the time up a bit. I'd like to spend the first portion of our time together learning about your background; then we'll turn it around to give you a chance to ask about us.

Playing Down Unfavorable Information

Whenever the applicant says something that is uncomfortable to admit, it is usually that very topic that the interviewer desires to hear more about. However, a direct question concerning the issue is likely to cause the applicant to raise his guard and to give an answer that seems reasonable, prudent, and logical but perhaps is not a true depiction of the actual situation. Most candidates will not speak freely about a negative point if they think that the interviewer regards the point as highly important or significant. In fact, the more attention the interviewer gives to a negative issue, the more cautious the applicant will be in talking about it. Thus it is usually desirable to play down unfavorable information when it is heard.

The easiest way to play down a statement is to indicate that it is a common experience for others. If, for instance, the applicant says that he or she was let go from a summer job because of a personality conflict with the boss, the interviewer might encourage a further explanation of that topic by playing down the applicant's statement. He might say, "Well, there is hardly a person working today who hasn't run into a boss like that at some time or another during a business career. What happened in this particular instance?" Or the applicant might indicate that he failed analytical geometry in college. The interviewer could say, "Well, I know that was a dog course when I went to school. What gave you a little trouble when you were taking it?" In other words, it is important to let applicants know that they can safely talk about shortcomings without the interviewer becoming negatively prejudiced.

Another way to make a negative issue less threatening is to ask the candidate a question that does not imply negative judgment but is still related to the issue at hand. For instance, the interviewer could ask, "What, if anything, would you say you learned from that experience?"

It is also helpful to express to the applicant your appreciation for the honesty and frankness shown. If the interviewer makes a statement such as, "I really appreciate your frankness in mentioning that point. I'm sure it wasn't easy for you to bring it up," quite often the applicant picks up the conversation and elaborates further on the matter.

When you make an effort to play down negative input but notice that the applicant is still defensive and reluctant to talk, the subject can be temporarily dropped. It should be brought up later, near the end of the interview. Please note, however, that it is scarcely less threatening to the applicant when it is raised at a later point in the discussion. Threatening material should be discussed, if at all possible, at the time it is first mentioned.

Avoiding Disagreement

Disagreement with a candidate's statement signals to the applicant that the "wrong thing" was said. Thus if more information is desired, the interviewer should not express disapproval or disagreement. This does not mean, however, that the interviewer needs to compromise principles or agree with points of view contrary to one's beliefs. It simply means that it is necessary to avoid disagreeing or showing disapproval. For example, if a college recruit said he thought that "American business today exploits young college graduates and doesn't allow them to use their capabilities," and the interviewer wants to learn the rationale behind the applicant's views, he might respond in a neutral tone, "Well that's an interesting comment, let's talk a little bit about it."

Sincere Compliments

One of the easiest—and yet most neglected—approaches an interviewer can take to reduce threat and anxiety is to give sincere praise of an applicant's achievements. For example, if an interview has revealed that an applicant earned spending money since the age of ten years, the interviewer might say, "You must be proud of that." Or the interviewer could simply say, "Good," or "That kind of trait should be a great asset at work."

The reader is cautioned not to flatter or insincerely praise the candidate. Flattery will be perceived as phony and unrealistic. It is a rare candidate, however, who does not have some achievements that are truly praiseworthy and about which positive comments can be made. The commendation should be simple, straightforward, and not flowery.

It is interesting to note the reaction of applicants when they are praised. Beneath the surface, the applicant usually experiences a feeling of greater self-confidence in the interview situation. This increase in confidence sometimes can be observed in external behavior. Most applicants will begin to slouch, ever so slightly, in their chairs once a sincere compliment has been paid to them.

The interviewer should create a climate in which the applicant feels he or she is making a favorable impression. When this occurs, the candidate will be more self-assured, relaxed, and willing to share openly—sometimes even willing to share some shortcoming. This is likely to occur, however, only when the interviewer provides positive feedback that the candidate's accomplishments are well regarded. In contrast, the applicant who feels he or she is not making a favorable impression or is uncertain about the impact being made, is likely to become tense and more cautious about what is said, making it all the more difficult to elicit sensitive information.

Threatening Questions

While the primary theme of this chapter is the need to keep a low-threat climate throughout the interview, it should be recognized that there are times when threat cannot be avoided. The interviewer should not leave unresolved questions if an answer can be determined by more thorough exploration or more probing questions.

In such instances, the applicant will be put on the spot and the threat level significantly increased.

Suppose, for example, the applicant has a record of frequent job changes. Over the past six years, he has changed jobs three times—almost once every two years. The applicant in every other respect seems to be an ideal choice for the job, but the question that keeps going through the interviewer's mind is whether or not the applicant will leave this company after two years. If no clear-cut answer to that concern is gleaned during the course of the interview, then the interviewer should focus his attention directly on it.

INTERVIEWER: Mr. Jones, after reviewing your background, I feel you might be a very fine candidate for the opening we have. However, the one thought that keeps going through my mind is that you left your last three companies after only a two-year stay. Since we're going to invest so much time and expense in training you, I'm concerned about the possibility that you might leave us after a short period of time. Are there any reasons I should believe you might not leave us, as you did the other companies?

Another example of a situation in which pressure may be applied is when the interviewer gets the feeling that the applicant is a person who is fundamentally rather hostile— one who would react inappropriately when frustrated. Suppose the interviewer tried all sorts of indirect ways to obtain an understanding of how the candidate deals with frustrations but was unsuccessful. In such a case, the interviewer should not hesitate to put the applicant in a threatening position.

INTERVIEWER: We've been talking here now for almost thirty minutes and I can't help but get the feeling, as we discuss matters, that you might be the kind of person who walks around with a chip on the shoulder. How do you evaluate yourself on this score?

When there are some concerns or unresolved doubts, the interviewer should put them directly to the applicant and make the applicant prove to the interviewer's satisfaction whether or not the concerns are groundless.

The Place for Threat

When threat is purposely introduced in the interview, there is a definite time and place for it. That time and place is at about the three-quarter mark. Prior to the last fourth of the interview, effort should be made to play down unfavorable information and keep threat relatively low.

The strategy for coping with threat begins by keeping threat as low as possible throughout the interview. Wherever possible, use the play-down techniques to keep anxiety minimal. If this is not effective, withhold discussion of the point in question until later in the interview—at about the three-quarter point. At that time, weave the threatening issue into an exploration area that is somewhat related to it; that is, instead of dealing with this negative point in an isolated fashion, integrate it into the segment of the interview at the three-quarter mark.

After the threatening topic has been covered, the interviewer should attempt to reduce defensiveness by introducing a number of questions or topics that are relatively easy for the applicant to discuss. Questions that elicit positive answers are helpful here. For example, the interviewer could ask questions about how the applicant went about achieving some accomplishment or some activity.

Summary

It is recommended that the interviewer avoid trial behavior situations or stress interviews but rather seek open, frank, and revealing information by creating a climate that is relatively nonthreatening.

An environment that is relatively low in threat is achieved by showing a sincere interest in the applicant, playing down unfavorable information, avoiding disagreement with or disapproval of the applicant's statements, and by offering sincere praise and recognition of one's accomplishments. Open and free-flowing discussions are most likely to occur when the applicant feels he or she is about making a favorable impression on the interviewer. Then the applicant may be more willing to discuss unfavorable aspects about self or background. When threatening topics must be discussed, they should be raised at the three-quarter mark in the interview, not at the beginning or end.

CHAPTER 5

Learning About Others— How to Encourage Applicants to Talk

The value of a nonthreatening climate to encourage the applicant to be frank about shortcomings as well as strengths has been discussed. However, proper climate is not sufficient to keep the applicant talking. The interviewer needs to employ techniques that will help the interview become a smooth-flowing conversation rather than a question-and-answer period. Ideally, the applicant should move freely from topic to topic, freely associating one idea after the other. The exact manner in which the interviewer achieves this and yet keeps control of the interview will be discussed later. First, however, the interviewer needs to know ways to draw out the discussion on points of interest to the interviewer.

Listening Techniques

It should be understood that people will usually talk to the degree that they believe you are interested and want to hear what they have to say. Applicants will talk to the degree that you will listen. Thus, effective use of listening techniques is critical to good interviewing.

Five basic techniques are available to the interviewers to help the applicant verbalize freely.

1. Open-ended questions.
2. Accepting the applicant.
3. Restating or reflecting.
4. Pause or silence.
5. Nonverbals.

These tools of the trade have broad application for the manager whether in employment interviewing, job coaching, or trying to understand the objections someone has to an idea. The tools for listening are well worth mastering. These techniques are not designed to stand alone but rather to be intermingled with one another. The precise manner in which they are used depends upon the nature of the material being covered, the sensitivity of the topic being discussed, and the style of the interviewer. In most interviews, all five techniques are used together to create an atmosphere that encourages the applicant to verbalize freely and to elaborate on important issues.

Open-Ended Questions

The most frequently used of all talk-generating techniques is asking questions. Interviewers should avoid closed-ended questions that lead simply to a yes or no answer. In such cases, applicants often fail to elaborate and share meaningful information about themselves. A typical closed-ended question would be "Did you like your last job?" In contrast, notice how the open-ended question elicits much more information, "What were some of the things about your last job that were appealing to you?" In this particular example, the interviewer may receive several answers that will help in understanding the motivations of the candidate.

Most open-ended questions begin with *what, why, how,* or *tell me.*

Starting questions with the following words will usually produce a closed-ended question and a limited response from the candidate: *do, have, is, was, would, did, had, are, were,* and *could.* There are other closed-ended beginning words, but these are the most common.

Open-ended questions are particularly useful in starting off the exploration of the life areas that should be covered in the interview. Open-ended questions, which are broad in nature, are sometimes referred to as broad-brush questions. A typical open-ended statement designed to initiate discussion of a life area is, "Let's go on now and *tell me* something about your job experiences."

The importance of using open-ended questions cannot be overstressed. Some specific values come from their use apart from the fact that the applicant verbalizes more freely. Such a question tells the applicant that you are interested in what he or she has to say. In effect, it says to the applicant, "I care about your ideas. I recognize that what you think is important, and because of that I'm willing to give you the freedom to flesh out the answer as you choose."

Also, it allows the interviewer to learn not only about the content but also about *how* the applicant responds. For example, how well does the applicant structure or not structure his answer? Is his answer scattered, systematic, terse, relaxed, superficial, or complete? As much can be learned from the applicant's *way* of answering as can be learned from the reply. Also, the open-ended question usually creates a relatively nondefensive climate; it gives applicants opportunity to structure their answers in their own manner.

Problems with Use of Questions

Even if the interviewer uses many open-ended questions, consistent or exclusive use of questions for obtaining interview data is not recommended. As was suggested in the beginning of this section, use of a variety of interviewing tools is most effective. However, because so many interviewers find questions the most natural way of eliciting data, there is a tendency (particularly with beginning interviewers) to rely too much on them. Let's examine, for a moment, some of the difficulties encountered if questions become the primary means of encouraging the applicant to talk.

Reduced input from the applicant. There is significant evidence to suggest that the amount of verbal response from an applicant diminishes in proportion to the number of questions asked in a series. If the interviewer asks several questions, one after the other, the likelihood is that the applicant will give shorter and shorter responses to each succeeding question.

The failure of the applicant to elaborate occurs because, in effect, the applicant perceives the interviewer as saying, "Look, there are some important things I want to know, and if I want to know them, I'll ask you."

It is important that the interviewer does not cut off or discourage elaborations by the applicant. It is through these somewhat gratuitous comments that the interviewer begins to hear thoughts that have not been carefully prescreened by the applicant. As interviewers, we want the applicant to free associate, to ramble a bit, and to enlarge upon responses.

May put the applicant on the defensive. At its worst, questioning can become an inquisition and cut off almost all conversation. At its best, questioning tends to arouse caution in the applicant. Whenever the interviewer asks a question, the applicant understands that the topic is one of importance to the interviewer. Thus applicants tend to be more careful in the selection of their words and the manner in which they respond.

Makes it easy to be fooled. The extensive use of questions makes it easy for the applicant to look good. In effect, when interviewers rely on questions, the interview becomes a series of discrete thought units. Here is a typical example.

INTERVIEWER: How were your grades in college?

APPLICANT: Oh, pretty good. I was in the upper third of my class and I made the dean's list last semester.

INTERVIEWER: How about extracurricular activities—were you involved in any?

APPLICANT: Well, I was quite active. I got a letter in track and was active in intramurals. In fact, our fraternity won the softball league championship. I also belonged to the radio club and was chairman of the soph hop.

It can readily be seen that for each question the applicant has the opportunity to select a reaction; the applicant is given the opportunity and time to analyze the question, sift through alternative answers, and pick the one that will put him or her in the best possible light. One can also note, from the foregoing dialog, it is quite evident to this applicant that extracurricular activities are important to the interviewer. Consequently, he strives hard to resurrect as many positive facts as he can.

It is interesting to contrast this question approach with normal conversation in which the participants tend to exchange ideas, building one thought upon the other. The interviewer will learn much more about how candidates think and behave during a relatively unstructured conversation than if applicants are given the opportunity through questions to carefully select those responses that will make them look good.

Burdening the interviewer. A final problem with reliance on questions as the central technique for soliciting information is the burden it puts on the interviewer. Most inexperienced interviewers have the problem of trying to know what to ask next. Many interviewers become so preoccupied with formulating the right questions that little time is left to analyze the answers or obtain a meaningful understanding of the individual in front of them. Questions are helpful in controlling the discussion but need to be used in conjunction with other techniques.

It should also be recognized that the interviewer who relies on questions to stimulate discussion assumes he knows the right questions to ask. He inquires about the topics he believes are relevant, but in so doing he may overly control the interview and divert time and attention away from other unthought of, but meaningful, elements in the applicant's background.

Accepting the Applicant

Another tool that aids listening, and at the same time encourages conversation, is to accept what is being said rather than either condemning it or condoning it. Acceptance is shown by use of such statements as "Uh-huh,"

"Go on," "I see," "I understand," "That's interesting," or any other short acknowledgment of understanding.

These statements say, in a sense, "I'm interested, go on with what you're saying." Almost anyone who is skillful in conversation uses acceptance comments as a means of encouraging elaboration of a point of view.

Restating and Reflecting

Conversation is stimulated when the interviewer shows understanding of the applicant's statement. The interviewer accomplishes this by listening to a statement by the applicant and then mirroring back in his own words his understanding of what was said. This technique can be called rephrasing or restating, terms that will be used interchangeably. For example:

INTERVIEWER: Do you see any possible difficulties you might have in getting started on this job?

APPLICANT: Well, the only possible difficulty I can see is that I would have to go slow at first, at least until I got a little more familiar with the exact way you people operate.

INTERVIEWER: [Rephrasing] You would tend to start off slowly and then pick up speed as you get more familiar with the work.

APPLICANT: Yes, I guess that's right. I like to be pretty sure of myself before I really take over the full operation of a machine. Besides, the kind of equipment we had at the other company isn't exactly the same type you have here—I guess I'm not as familiar with your kind of process as I should be.

Here is another example of restating.

INTERVIEWER: What would you say might be some of your shortcomings?

APPLICANT: I really can't think of any significant shortcomings I have. Whenever I felt I was weak in something, I worked hard to overcome it.

INTERVIEWER: [Rephrasing] You feel then that there really aren't any things you could improve very much upon.

APPLICANT: Well, of course, I couldn't say that. I guess everybody can improve in some things.

INTERVIEWER: [Rephrasing] There might be some things you could possibly do better in.

APPLICANT: Well, as I said, yes. I guess everybody can improve somewhat. The only thing that I can really point to is the fact that I. . . .

The rephrasing promotes meaningful discussion because the interviewer is attempting to understand what the applicant is saying. In most cases, restatements should not prove threatening to the applicant who has already said whatever is being rephrased. Restating, in effect, says, "I'm interested; I'm trying to understand; the door's open for you to tell me more if you want to." Usually, candidates accept the invitation to expand on the point they have just made.

A more sophisticated version of restating is called reflecting; that is, the interviewer reflects back the feelings and attitudes that are being expressed rather than words themselves. For example:

APPLICANT: [Angrily] In XYZ Company, they just let people go without any reason or cause.

INTERVIEWER: [Reflects feeling] It makes you angry even to think about it.

APPLICANT: You bet it does! There was only one time when I ever got out of line in that company and that was when. . . .

A second example demonstrates the value of the technique in acquiring information in a sensitive area.

APPLICANT: I just don't think your question is an appropriate one to ask in an employment interview.

INTERVIEWER: [Reflecting feeling] You feel a little uncomfortable talking about your reasons for resigning.

APPLICANT: Well, I guess you're right. I probably do feel uncomfortable because . . . Oh, what the hell, I might as well tell you. My boss and I really had a personality conflict and. . . .

In these examples, it is probably apparent that the interviewer could have elicited further information about the applicant's statements simply by asking a question. If this procedure were followed, however, the applicant would clearly have been put on the spot and probably would have become quite defensive. Defensiveness is not usually aroused by restating or reflecting. The interviewer is not criticizing, not approving, not disapproving, and not making the person justify his statement. Restating shows interest, but above all it displays a sense of understanding.

It might be worthwhile to comment here that other than restating or rephrasing there are no convincing ways in which understanding can be communicated. To say to an individual that you are trying to understand the reasons why he changed jobs does not really convince him that you are attempting to understand. It is only by your actions that an applicant can be convinced of your sincerity. Restatement and reflection of feelings and attitudes, followed by listening, are the actions that show understanding. It is impossible for the interviewer to accurately rephrase or reflect if he has not listened and understood.

Intentional misstating. Sometimes interviewers will intentionally misstate an applicant's remark in order to test how strongly the applicant feels about a point of view. This procedure is not recommended. If the interviewer misstates too often, the applicant will feel that he is being toyed with, or he may conclude that the interviewer is stupid. At other times, the temptation to misstate stems from an assumption the interviewer has made about the applicant that he wants to confirm. For instance:

APPLICANT: I always look at things pretty carefully and weigh the long-term consequences of each decision.
INTERVIEWER: Sometimes you procrastinate until you feel you've got the correct solution.

To repeat, intentional misstating, except on rare occasions, is not advised. Instead, the interviewer should make an accurate restatement; as the applicant expands on the initial statement, the interviewer is likely to hear enough to help confirm or deny his hunch or assumption. To see how accurate restatement works, let us begin with the same example.

APPLICANT: I always look at things pretty carefully and weigh the long-term consequences of each decision.

INTERVIEWER: You're cautious in the way you go about making decisions.

APPLICANT: Yes, that's right. I feel that the time invested in making the right decision really has a pay-off when you compare it with the wasted effort that is required to undo a wrong decision. Of course, some people might call it procrastination, but I feel it's just good management.

Caution in use of the restatement. When managers learn to listen by restating, they often express concern that it will be too unnatural, that is, restating might sound unreal or phony. These fears are quite justified if the interviewer does not have a sincere desire to try to understand what it is that the applicant is saying. If the restatement is made primarily to keep the conversation going and not to understand, the applicant will feel he is being "techniqued." It cannot be overemphasized that restatement and reflection will be effective to stimulate discussion only if the user is sincerely interested in the other person's point of view.

There will be times, however, even when understanding is the intent of the manager, that the restating method does not seem to work. The applicant does not continue the dialog or expand upon the topic at hand. If the interviewer encounters silence or simply a no or yes answer after restating, two basic causes for this lack of verbalization should be considered. First, the interviewer may have restated something that was too simple and matter-of-fact. For example:

APPLICANT: It sure is warm out there today.
INTERVIEWER: You feel it's quite hot.
APPLICANT: Yeah, that's what I said.

A second instance in which rephrasing may fail is when the interviewer makes a question of the restatement by putting an inflection on the last word of the sentence. The most effective way to rephrase or to express the thought is in a flat, declarative manner without the inflection that turns the period into a question mark.

In the overview, restatement and reflection have their greatest value when the topic being discussed is touchy, sensitive, or conflict laden. Here is an example of a situation in which restating is appropriate.

APPLICANT: Well, to be quite frank with you, I really was fired from that summer job.

INTERVIEWER: Something led your boss to think that you weren't quite suited for the job.

APPLICANT: Well, I never really thought of it that way, but I guess that was the case. You see, I never really did enjoy. . . .

In this situation the use of questions would be relatively unproductive. The natural tendency, of course, is to ask, "Well, what caused them to let you go?" When such a question is voiced, however, the applicant is aware of the significance that will be attached to the answer. As a result, he or she will be careful to pick and choose a response that will sound prudent and reasonable. With restatement, the topic is kept open so that the applicant can discuss it in a less defensive manner.

Pause or Silence

One of the most powerful tools in an interviewer's repertoire is the use of a pause or silence. Whenever two or more persons are engaged in a conversation and a pause occurs, tremendous psychological pressure is built up to fill the conversational gap. Because the interviewer should feel more secure in his role than the applicant, the pressure to speak is far greater for the candidate than for the interviewing manager. This is one reason the pause technique works. Silence also asks, without the use of words, "Well, what else can you add?" Silence or pause suggests to the applicant that more is expected.

The use of silence, however, carries with it the inherent problem of threat. As was discussed earlier threat is more likely to discourage free-flowing conversation than to encourage it. Thus silence can be misused and abused. There are, however, two occasions in which silence can be used effectively without accompanying threat or discomfort.

First, pause is most effective after the interviewer has asked a question. When a question is addressed to anyone, it is clearly understood that it is the other person's turn to speak. However, whenever the applicant does not immediately answer the question asked, most interviewers jump into the discussion and answer the question themselves. Sometimes interviewers clarify their questions with additional statements.

There is no real justification for the interviewer to continue to speak once he has asked a question. It cannot be assumed that just because the applicant is silent nothing is going on. He or she may be thinking through what to say or how to phrase the answer. It is often after such pauses that the most significant comments are spoken. There is a similarity here between the interview and psychotherapy. In verbal therapy, the most important insights do not necessarily come as the patient is conversing freely with the therapist but rather after a period of silence. During this silence, the patient is usually wrestling with the problem of whether or not to reveal to the therapist a certain element in background or makeup. Eventually, the person blurts it out. Thus information coming after a period of silence often is far more meaningful and relevant than information that springs from a fast-moving discussion.

At this point, some managers may still wonder if pausing after asking a question may not result in stress and discomfort for the applicant. The answer must be no, because it is not the interviewer who is now creating silence but the applicant. The candidate to whom the question is addressed knows, as well as the interviewer, that it is now his or her turn to speak. The fact that one does not speak suggests an attempt to decide what to share with the interviewer rather than a decision not to answer the question. The silence, if it persists, is actually being sustained by the applicant. After all, the applicant can break the silence any time by a limitless range of comments. For example, one could say, "I don't quite understand what you mean," or "I want to think about it a little bit before I answer that question."

If the applicant does not break the silence, there is little or no value in the interviewer's doing it. It is not necessary to stare down the applicant, but rather the interviewer should try to communicate in a nonverbal manner (sitting back in

the chair, for example) that he realizes the applicant is thinking through the answer.

A second occasion in which the pause can be helpful and
yet nonthreatening is when the pause is of relatively short
duration. These pauses are best used once the person has
completed a thought or answered a question. For example:

INTERVIEWER: How did things go with you over at ABC
Company?
APPLICANT: OK, we had our ups and downs, but generally,
I'd say OK.
INTERVIEWER: [Pauses five or six seconds]
APPLICANT: Well, actually he wasn't the kind of person I like
working for. . . . He. . . .

Tape recordings reveal that when the pause is used after
the applicant has made a statement the applicant often adds
something. He says, for example, "And another thing. . . ."
Or he will say, "I'll tell you something else. . . ."

If this process is examined, it is easy to understand why
applicants add meaningful comments after a pause even
though it appears that they have finished. While responding
to a question, the applicant is simultaneously filtering, cen-
soring, and organizing thoughts and pondering whether or
not to reveal them. When the pause occurs at this point,
there is a strong likelihood that the applicant will decide to
share the thought with the interviewer. One almost feels
compelled to go on and then says, "The other thing about
that is. . . ."

The interviewer who jumps in as soon as the applicant
has finished a statement will be cutting off all chance of hearing any addendum. Thus good interviewing, like good listening, is typically slow-paced. There is no need for the interviewer to worry about having a probing question to ask next
or responding in a witty or highly intelligent manner. The
interviewer should relax and pace the discussion at a comfortable rate. Pauses of short duration during the interview
are not going to create problems and may, indeed, help the
interviewer learn many meaningful things that otherwise
would have been unspoken.

Nonverbals

Another important tool that helps keep the applicant talking is the appropriate use of nonverbal cues. Often, more information is communicated through nonverbals than by words. An interviewer can say, "I'm very interested in what happened on that job," but, at the same time, his or her gestures, or frowns, or body postures, might clearly indicate boredom or lack of interest. It is important, therefore, that the interviewer pay attention to the nonverbal cues he or she provides the applicant.

A helpful nonverbal is to nod understandingly at the completion of a statement by the applicant. Interviewers can also lean forward, show attention, and use appropriate hand gestures. All of these cues show the interviewer's interest and encourage the applicant to continue talking.

A question often arises about the nonverbal matter of eye contact. If the interviewer continually focuses attention out the window, or on the wall, or on a notepad, it will be distracting to the applicant and is likely to be interpreted as indifference. On the other hand, constant eye contact can often become quite uncomfortable; the interviewer should not try to engage in a staring contest. Instead, occasional eye contact is recommended. It helps build rapport and shows the candidate that he or she has the attention of the interviewer.

Interviewers would also be well advised to try to avoid distracting nonverbal gestures, such as toying with pencils, slouching in chairs, rattling papers, or picking lint off their clothes. All these actions say to applicants that the interviewer's attention is elsewhere and not focused on them.

Nonverbals show applicants how they are "coming across." The occasional smile, the hand gesture, the nod of the head all say, in effect, "Hey, I'm interested, I'm with you, and I'm listening." In contrast, when the interviewer shows no overt nonverbal behavior, but instead is somewhat fixed and immobile, it is difficult for the candidate to understand the impact of statements upon the interviewer. This unknown makes the applicant uncomfortable and will make it difficult for the interviewer to establish easy rapport with the candidate.

Another aspect of nonverbals has to do with proximity of

the interviewer to the applicant. The extent to which physical closeness and touching of applicants are acceptable and desirable varies greatly with the candidate's cultural background. The safest stance for the interviewer is to shake hands at the beginning and the end of the interview and try to be sensitive to the applicant's desire for any further contact of this sort. Generally, it is recommended that the physical distance between the interviewer and the applicant be not more than five feet and not less than two feet. It is usually desirable to provide some safe territory for the candidate and not suggest too much familiarity.

Summary

Five basic techniques—questions, accepting, rephrasing, pausing, and nonverbals—have been outlined as tools for listening and for keeping the interview moving on a conversational plane. The question usually serves as the interviewer's control device. It determines the topic to be discussed. The five techniques are then used together to draw out the applicant on the topic at hand until sufficient information has been gathered.

It is not good interview technique to extensively use any one of the five devices to the exclusion of the others. This is particularly true with questions. Restating is best used in discussing topics that are sensitive or threatening.

The listening techniques described in this chapter are the tools of interviewing. Their effectiveness, however, depends, above all, upon a true desire to really want to listen.

CHAPTER 6

How to Evaluate
What You Hear—
A Conceptual Viewpoint

For almost every interviewer, the most frustrating and difficult aspect of interviewing is evaluating data—putting meaning on what is seen and heard. Part of the interviewer's difficulty stems from his or her focus on obtaining more information instead of concentrating on the meaning of the data already in hand. Another evaluation problem stems from the lack of an effective system by which to correctly interpret the facts already gathered. Let's examine each of these problems in a little more depth.

The Need to Shift the Focus from Facts to Causes

Most interviewers finish the interview with more data than when they start. But even though they have more facts, they rarely have a good understanding of how the applicant will perform on the job. Yet, isn't that the primary purpose of the interviewer—to use past and present behavior as a basis for predicting future performance? The gathering of more facts is usually not what is required to make this prediction; rather it is the translation of the facts into meaningful job behavior.

76

If several managers are given a one-page résumé covering the usual background data about an individual and are then asked if they would make a hire, not-hire decision on the basis of the résumé, the usual answer is no. If asked why not, they respond with statements such as "I don't know what his personality is like. Is he shy? Confident? Aggressive? Or what?" "I don't know how he would interact with me. Will I be able to get along well with him?" "He indicates he changed from a major in accounting to one in engineering. I wonder if he really knows what he wants to do?" "I wonder why he didn't take a summer job during his junior year?"

Give the same group another résumé, but this time include more facts about the individual's work experience, education, and the like, and ask the same question. As before, the managers will give a no response. And the reasons will be the same—basically they want to know more about what lies behind the facts. Why did the person do certain things? What was the motivation involved? What is he like from the personality standpoint? What is his appearance? What are his motives? What accounted for his success or failure in various situations? In other words, in most interview situations, the interviewer does not need more historical facts than the application blank provides, but rather needs to interpret the facts already available.

Need for Interpretation System

A second factor that makes interpretation of data so difficult is that most interviewers have not developed or learned about a system for evaluating data. To be effective, such a system must be able to help solve three significant problems that affect objective evaluation of candidates. These problems are (1) overcontrolling or overstructuring the interview, thus narrowing the range of observations and data obtained; (2) jumping to conclusions about the meaning of the data, resulting in an incorrect interpretation, and (3) failing to convert the facts of the applicant's background into meaningful behavior terms. Instead, the interviewer interprets data as being essentially favorable or unfavorable, and the applicant with the most favorables and least unfavorables usually gets accepted, even though the interviewer cannot describe how the candidate will perform on the job.

To help analyze data, this chapter and Chapter 7 present procedures that consist of two key elements. The first procedure has to do with how to conduct the interview efficiently so that the data sources are not narrow or circumscribed. This conceptual approach to the interview will be referred to as the *emergence approach.* The second is a specific technique to help avoid jumping to conclusions and to provide an accurate interpretation of what is seen and heard during the interview. This technique will be referred to as the *hypothesis method,* to be discussed in Chapter 7.

The Emergence Approach

The emergence approach is really a philosophical attitude or mentality about how the interviewer perceives his or her role in gathering data—a role in which the interviewer helps applicants reveal themselves, rather than having the interviewer directly seek out behavior patterns.

The emergence approach is based on the principle of human behavior that says if you give people enough latitude to talk about themselves, to let them be themselves, then their day-in, day-out, typical behavior patterns (personality, motivation, and thinking patterns) will rise to the surface.

It doesn't matter a great deal exactly what is covered in an interview; if the applicant talks freely for a sufficient length of time, the interviewer will learn a tremendous amount about that person. The emergence principle can also be observed in social situations. Suppose, for instance, you go to a party or business meeting at which most of the people are strangers to you. How do you decide whether or not you would like to be together again with someone you meet? Do you interview them? Of course not; you talk. What do you talk about? Usually nothing in particular, maybe whatever the other person brings up. But as you listen and observe, you hear attitudes conveyed, you get some "feel" for how smart a person is, personality traits and behaviorisms are projected, and interests are mentioned. You haven't structured a list of topics to discuss or probe, but simply by letting other persons "be" and project themselves, you can learn much about them.

Interviewers can readily learn about others through careful observation, because anything people do represents an extension of their basic selves—how they walk, how they talk, how they laugh, how they handwrite—all reveal something of the inner person. When this principle is applied to the interview situation, it suggests that if we truly want to learn how someone else behaves and functions, then we, as interviewers, should provide a lot of freedom to let the interviewees "be." We should begin the interview with an open mind and not search for anything in particular. Obviously, it is necessary, during an employment interview, to explore whether or not the candidate has the necessary technological skills or experiences (knowledge-experience factor) to perform the job for which he or she is being considered. Therefore, opportunity will be provided, when necessary, to explore and probe for specific factual data. However, when the interviewer is attempting to learn about the candidate, in the more difficult-to-assess factors (intellect, motivation, and personality), use of the emergence principle is essential. Thus, a small portion of the interview is relegated to the exploration of specific information, but for the major portion of the interview time, the interviewer should try to determine what the candidate is like, rather than searching out specific qualities, traits, or behaviorisms.

Basically, the emergence approach suggests that when you conduct the interview, you search out nothing (except when exploring for knowledge and experience data), but instead, see what emerges. The interviewer should try to understand how the candidate functions—how he or she solves problems, relates to others, is motivated, and applies aptitudes and skills. Once the interviewer has developed a mental portrait of how the applicant behaves and functions, then, and only then, should the interviewer relate the emerged qualities to the behaviors critical to success on the job.

Problems with Traditional Methods of Interviewing

As you already may have concluded, the emergence approach is completely contrary to the classical approach to interviewing. The traditional wisdom in conducting the interview is to identify what is needed for success on the job, and then attempt to determine if the applicant possesses those particular skills, traits, and abilities. An examination of the "let's-see-if-the-candidate-has-what-we-want" approach reveals a number of significant reasons that interviewers should look to alternative methods of conducting the interview, such as the emergence approach.

Obvious Intent

Chapter 2, "Problems in Interviewing," discussed the issue of "telegraphing" the right responses. This problem becomes acute when the interviewer tries to ferret out a specific kind of information about the applicant. In most cases, if the interviewer looks hard enough, the sought-after quality will be found, whether the candidate possesses the ability or not. Most applicants are sufficiently perceptive to see exactly what is being searched out and, if the quality is desirable, they will indicate that they have it.

Limited Validity of Behavioral Traits

As was mentioned earlier, many personnel evaluation procedures concentrate on finding someone who has a certain set of traits, qualities, or abilities that are needed for success on a given job. On the surface, such an approach seems logical. As we watch successful people perform in different assignments, we do occasionally notice that the more effective ones tend to be decisive, or forceful, or intelligent, or to demonstrate some other trait. The assumption is then made that to identify successful employees for that job those qualities must also be found in the applicants. Applicants who do not seem to possess these few qualities are eliminated from further consideration.

An extension of the traits approach can often be found on interviewer guide sheets. These forms usually list ten or twelve traits upon which the candidate is to be rated. The assumption in using such guide sheets is that these traits account for the success or failure of job incumbents. An example of a portion of this type of interview evaluation guide is shown in Figure 5.

However, there is serious doubt that any particular set of traits or qualities is necessary for success in any particular job. Rarely does research reveal a clear-cut pattern or profile for successful people in professional or managerial assignments. While it is quite possible, of course, for psychologists to establish patterns for positions with clearly defined responsibilities, such data do not exist in most companies.

It should be recognized that the combinations and permutations of individuals' talents, skills, and abilities are almost limitless. It is the complexity of the human being that continues to make the process of assessment (and management, too) both an art and a challenge. As a result, rarely can we be sure that a particular profile or set of qualities really accounts for success in a given job.

Moreover, even when research effort proves the validity of certain predictors, those validities often dramatically change over time. What may predict successfully today may not do so tomorrow.

Uniqueness of Individuals

It is a truism that everyone is unique. Yet, despite our awareness of this fact, most approaches to evaluating others run counter to the uniqueness concept. Think of some job in your organization in which several people have the same job titles. Let us assume further that those incumbents are all reasonably successful in performing their work. Are these people all the same? Probably not. In fact, in most cases, they will be quite different in many respects. It's not their sameness that makes them successful, but the unique blend of qualities and skills they bring to the job.

Compensating Strengths

Even if it were established that a particular ability or quality was important for success in a position, it could well be that that particular trait or quality would not have to manifest itself for every applicant to be effective on the job. A

FIGURE 5. Interview rating form focusing on traits (not recommended).

	Not ascertained; Don't know	1	2	3	4	5
ASSERTIVENESS	Not ascertained; Don't know	Easily discouraged; passive; tends to react to events; avoids challenging situations				Initiates activities; continues at tasks despite problems and setbacks; confident; seeks new and challenging situations
COMMUNICATION SKILLS	Not ascertained; Don't know		Hesitant and uncertain; has difficulty presenting ideas clearly and logically			Poised, confident and convincing; can present complex ideas in a clear and interesting manner
DECISIVENESS	Not ascertained; Don't know		Uncertain, ill-at-ease about decisions, frequently changes mind, takes excessive time to make decisions			Confident about decisions; accurately assesses risks and implications; makes decisions within appropriate time frame
ENERGY	Not ascertained; Don't know		Rarely works hard; appears to have difficulty maintaining a heavy workload and performing efficiently			Frequently works hard; capable of maintaining a heavy workload while remaining efficient
FLEXIBILITY	Not ascertained; Don't know		Unaware, oblivious of changing situations; has difficulty adapting and changing goals, directions, etc.			Sensitive to changing situations, capable of adapting to changing demands, goals, requirements, etc.
INTERPERSONAL SKILLS	Not ascertained; Don't know		Has difficulty maintaining relationships; insensitive; lacks tact			Capable of working effectively with others; sensitive to the feelings of others; tactful
MATURITY	Not ascertained; Don't know		Responds carelessly and impulsively; avoids assuming responsibility for own actions; panics under pressure			Carefully considers effects of potential actions; reliable; willingly accepts responsibility for handling difficult problems; calm under pressure
REASONING/JUDGMENT	Not ascertained; Don't know		Doesn't seek enough information; misses essentials of problem; solutions are superficial			Identifies need for and seeks relevant information; solutions have been innovative and effective

person could possess different combinations of strengths that would enable him or her to perform the same task quite effectively.

Suppose, for example, it is agreed that self-starting ability is an important requirement for a particular position in your firm. If self-starting initiative is not in evidence, an applicant is likely to be rejected. This focus, however, ignores the observation of other desirable factors. It may be that a candidate with a good record attributes success to conscientiousness, persistence, and a high energy level. Such a candidate could well become an excellent employee because of persistence and energy, even though goals must be set for him or her. If a superior is willing to set priorities and targets, this applicant could be a highly effective employee—without self-starting ability.

Undesirable Side of Traits

The traits or pattern approach tends to focus on desired traits for any given job but usually fails to evaluate their potential as undesirable characteristics. Interviewers who focus on trying to determine whether or not a given candidate has a certain set of qualities usually fail to consider the complexity of the human being and the interaction of the traits upon one another. For example, suppose that for a particular position it has been found that the best performers are socially aggressive; that is, they are forceful, dynamic individuals, particularly in face-to-face situations. Most interviewers would tend to perceive aggressiveness as desirable when they encounter it in an applicant. However, this very trait of aggressiveness could become a problem if the candidate is also a hostile person. In such a case, the more social aggressiveness displayed by the individual, the more likely is behavior likely to create problems, for both the employee and the company. Thus, the traits approach directs attention away from an understanding of other qualities that the individual possesses—many of which inhibit effective performance.

Notice, it's not that we don't want to know whether or not the applicant is aggressive, but precisely because we do want to learn, as accurately as possible, just how aggressive the individual is that we avoid searching it out and let the emergence principle operate.

If the applicant is truly aggressive, and the interviewer follows the procedures described in the evaluation model (Chapter 9), then clear-cut evidence of this aggressiveness should emerge from the discussion of the applicant's background. If the candidate is not aggressive, evidence of passive behavior should appear; if the candidate is neither aggressive nor unaggressive but middle-of-the-road on this quality, that also should be evident.

The point here is that no one quality, skill, or trait has much significance in and of itself; it is only analysis of the *total person* as to how and when these qualities are used that determines anyone's effectiveness in a given job.

The Emergence Approach and Conduct of the Interview

At this point, it may appear that some amorphous, tell-me-about-your-life kind of interview is being advocated. While such an approach could be very effective, time constraints make this kind of an interview impractical in most instances. Instead, we propose a rather structured format that permits the interviewer to control the interview and, at the same time, allows applicants sufficient freedom to project and reveal themselves to the interviewer.

It is critically important to understand the difference between going into the interview with an attitude that says, in effect, I will search out specific qualities that I deem are important to success in the job, and going into the interview with an open mind, relying on the emergence approach to reveal the nature of the applicant. In the latter case, the interviewer sets for himself or herself the goal of trying to determine how the candidate behaves or functions—how the person thinks, solves problems, and relates and deals with people, what turns him on and off, and how relevant their knowledge and experience are to the job in question. Once the interviewer understands and can describe the likely on-the-job behavior of the applicant, then the question can be asked, "If the individual functions this way, could this person do the job for which he or she is being assessed?" At this point, of course, technique ends and judgment begins. Then the interviewer must relate the behavioral patterns that emerged from the interview to the behavioral patterns required for successful performance of the job.

Keeping an Open Mind

Can the interviewer really be open-minded when conducting the interview? The answer to the question is yes, to a large degree. Interviewing is still a subjective process, and thus the application blank or résumé data, personal appearance, body language, and opinions of others all can contaminate the objectivity of an interviewer. So it is not possible to be completely open-minded and begin the interview with an entirely blank slate. On the other hand, it is quite another thing to purposely seek out (we are referring now to an evaluation interview, not simply a screening-out interview) predetermined qualities and attributes. Obviously, when it comes to assessing the applicant's technical knowledge or experience to do specific tasks, the interviewer must do a certain amount of searching and probing. In effect, the good interview utilizes the emergence approach about three-fourths of the time; one-fourth is allocated to determining if the applicant has adequate knowledge or experience to do the job.

Preinterview Data

If there is a significant advantage to conducting the interview with an open mind, using the emergence approach, then the question must be raised as to whether or not background data, such as application blanks or résumés, should be studied prior to the interview. The research on this question is ambiguous. For some interviewers, awareness of preinterview data enhanced their predictive accuracy; for others, it became a strong bias and disrupted ability to observe accurately.

There is no essential need to have preliminary data in

order to conduct a thorough and effective interview. However, if the interviewer feels it is of help to understand beforehand the track record of the applicant, it would be difficult to make a strong case against looking over the information before the interview. The danger is that if such preliminary reading contains negative information (reference comments, test scores, and so forth), odds are high that a negative bias will operate throughout the interview and will significantly disrupt the interviewer's objectivity. Not to expose oneself to data about the applicant prior to the interview seems the safest course. Negative data obtained after the interview is completed tends to have a less biasing effect.[1]

It is definitely recommended not to have the application blank or résumé in front of you as you interview. Such a practice tends to direct attention away from the applicant and toward the paper.

Problems arise when the interviewer refers frequently to a résumé or application blank during the interview. When a large array of information is directly in front of the interviewer, attentiveness to the applicant and motivation to carefully listen are substantially reduced. It is quite a different matter when the interviewer must draw all the information from the applicant; nothing can be assumed. Also, interviewers are subtly influenced by data in front of them. There is a tendency to assume that what is written is fact. Interviewers are inclined to overlook that many things happen in an applicant's life that never appear on a résumé. As a consequence, interviewers are less likely to ask such questions as, "Well, then what happened?" or, "What happened next?" In essence, the interviewer's chances of uncovering gaps in the candidate's background are sharply reduced.

When, at the outset of an interview, a job candidate stops the discussion to offer me a copy of his or her résumé, I usually reply, as I place it upside down on the desk, "Thank you very much. I'll study it later, but for now, I'd like to hear the story from you." Such a procedure has helped me do a

---

[1] See R. E. Carlson. "Effect of Interview Information in Altering Valid Impressions," *Journal of Applied Psychology*, Vol. 55, 1971, pp. 66–72.

better job in really getting to know the applicant, and it should work the same way for you.

Summary

During interviews, emphasis should be placed upon understanding the uniqueness of the individual being assessed rather than evaluating his sameness to others. This concept, called the emergence approach, dictates that the interviewer initiate the interview without a preconceived set of sought-after characteristics (with the exception of job knowledge); that is, the interviewer must not begin the interview with the intention of determining if the candidate possesses specific traits, qualities, aptitudes, or abilities. It is assumed that preliminary screening has eliminated those candidates whose educational background and work experience are inappropriate for the job in question. Consequently, the interviewer should try to understand how this person functions—how he or she solves problems, relates to others, is motivated, and applies aptitudes and skills. When the interviewer has developed a mental portrait of how the applicant behaves and functions, then, and only then, the interviewer can relate the emerging qualities to the requirements of the job.

Interviewers who follow the emergence approach will reduce the likelihood of seeing people as stereotypes, a trap into which so many interviewers fall. With the emergence approach, each individual is seen as unique—a more realistic viewpoint than classifying individuals after isolating a few behavior patterns. The emergence approach should also help the manager to work with the candidate once he or she is employed because the method yields an understanding of the dynamics of the individual.

Subsequent chapters will describe clear-cut steps as to how the emergence approach can be applied to the interview and how interviewing can be more easily accomplished with this method than with traits or pattern methods.

CHAPTER 7

How to Evaluate
What You Hear—
A Specific Method

The preceding chapter presented the emergence approach, an overall way of approaching the interview. Its primary purpose was to minimize the interviewer's preconceived notions and biases about what is important to seek out during the interview and, at the same time, allow applicants sufficient time and latitude to project their true qualities and behavior patterns. This chapter introduces a technique called the *hypothesis method*.

The Hypothesis Method

Basically, the hypothesis method is a technique used to assign meaning to data elicited from applicants or observed by interviewers. In effect, the method requires the interviewer to make a hypothesis, a guess if you will, as to what each input from the applicant will mean on the job. During the course of the interview, the interviewee will gather many of these hypotheses, perhaps thirty or forty; at the end of the interview, those hypotheses that repeat themselves will be accepted as true and meaningful behavioral characteristics of the individual being interviewed. By "repeat themselves" is meant that the same hypothesis emerges two, three, or four times during the course of the interview. Those hypotheses that are not confirmed are rejected. Out of the thirty or forty initial hypotheses developed, perhaps six, seven, or eight will remain as confirmed hypotheses. These will then be organized, at the end of the interview, into a balance sheet of principal strengths and weaknesses.

Briefly then, a large number of hypotheses are gathered. Those that are supported are taken to be true behavioral qualities of the applicant; those that are not supported are rejected.

Sources of Hypotheses

There are two basic sources from which the hypotheses are obtained: observed behavior and historical, factual data. By using the evaluation model described in Chapter 9, the interviewer will have ample opportunity to observe the candidate. The applicant can be observed as friendly, aggressive, nit-picking, conceptual, analytical, shy, hostile, confident, spontaneous, cool, distant, superficial, effecting good in self-expression, and so forth. Each time the interviewer observes a particular characteristic during the interview, a hypothesis can be made that that same behavior will manifest itself on the job. The observed behavior must be considered as hypothetical because the interview is only a sample of behavior. For example, just because an applicant is friendly in the interview, there is no guarantee that the same person will be friendly at work. However, the interviewer can hypothesize it will be so. Similarly, if someone is cautious and analytical during the interview, it is legitimate to hypothesize that he will be cautious and analytical on the job.

Whatever is observed—or whatever impressions the interviewer is receiving—are recorded as hypotheses (more about writing the hypotheses will be provided later). Note, too, that even fleeting hunches about the applicant should be recorded as hypotheses. Something that appears to be trivial and perhaps even irrelevant can have significance when additional, related hypotheses are gathered from subsequent portions of the interview. Remember, at this stage of the evaluation process, in which hypotheses are simply being assembled, they are regarded only as hypothetical, and not as true behavioral characteristics of the applicant.

The second source of the hypotheses stems from the historical data and factual information that are obtained as the interviewer explores an applicant's history—educational background, work experiences, leisure-time activities, and so on. Each time a fact is heard, the interviewer should make a hypothesis as to what that fact will mean on the job. For instance, suppose a female applicant indicates that she graduated from college in the upper 10 percent of her class. Let us assume further that she attended a relatively good school and that her class standing was verified. The hypothesis method now indicates that you should make a hypothesis as to what this particular historical fact will mean in terms of job behavior.

Most people, upon first hearing about the need to conjure a hypothesis each time a fact is heard, express a couple of concerns. The first has to do with the obvious difficulty of trying to formulate hypotheses in the midst of all else that is going on during the interview. What the interviewer is expected to do—control the interview, ask questions, listen, and also develop meaningful hypotheses—is a difficult task even for the professional interviewer. The executive with limited training in the behavioral sciences faces a more difficult task.

A second problem about trying to develop hypotheses from background data concerns whether or not one has the right hypothesis; that is, is the interviewer any further ahead than before formulating the hypothesis? This difficulty can be readily illustrated using the example about the applicant who said, "I graduated in the upper 10 percent of my class." During a recent presentation, I asked members of the audience what hypotheses they could think of that might explain this woman's good academic performance. Here are some of the hypotheses mentioned:

Bright, intelligent.
Competitive.
Strong need to achieve.
Conscientious—hard-working.

Learned how to be a student.
Cheated.
"Apple-polishes" her teachers.
Good study habits.
Self-disciplined—prepares well.
"Bookworm"—didn't do anything else but study.

I then turned to the group and asked, "Which one of these is correct?" Obviously, no one knew. All could have been correct, some could have been correct, or none could be right. And so, this hypothesis method immediately introduces two problems in its application: difficulty in formulating hypotheses especially under the pressure of the face-to-face interview, and in selecting the most correct of the many hypotheses that might occur to the interviewer.

Developing the Best Hypotheses

Fortunately, there is a tool at our disposal that simultaneously solves the two problems just mentioned. This tool is the self-appraisal question. Basically, the self-appraisal question asks the individual to explain in his or her own words the *how* or *why* of a piece of information. For example, suppose a male candidate indicates that he has been successful in selling *Time* magazine subscriptions while at college. A good self-appraisal question might be, "What did you do as a salesman that accounted for your fine sales record?" Or an applicant might indicate that he was the rush chairman for his fraternity. The interviewer then might ask, "What do you suppose it was that your fellow fraternity brothers saw in you that led them to pick you for rush chairman rather than some of the other fraternity members they might have selected?"

To return to our example of the woman who graduated in the upper 10 percent of her class, a self-appraisal question that could be asked follows.

INTERVIEWER: What is there about yourself that might account for the fine grades you obtained at the university?
APPLICANT: Well, I'm the kind of a person who likes to do things right. Do you know what I mean? When I decided to go to college, I planned on doing the best I could. I'll have to admit, I had to work hard for my grades—there

was many a weekend I stayed at school preparing for exams or writing term papers, but that's just how I am. I guess I'm just conscientious.

Now looking back at the list of hypotheses, it is clear that the probably correct one is "conscientious—hard-working." Of course, the woman's response about being hard-working might simply represent something the applicant made up because she thought it would sound good. Remember, however, as was mentioned earlier, that the applicant's response to the self-appraisal question is recorded only as a hypothesis. It is not accepted as being true until that same conscientiousness emerges from discussions about other segments of the applicant's life. If it recurs three or four times, it is reasonable to accept it as a true characteristic of the individual; if it does not appear meaningfully again, the hypothesis will not appear on the list of confirmed hypotheses. After all, if an individual is truly hard-working and conscientious, it doesn't manifest itself for just a moment and not ever again. If the behavior is at all meaningful in the individual's makeup, it should reappear in other aspects of the person's life, provided, of course, that one conducts the interview so as to allow the person to reveal himself as he explains about life experiences.

Some Advantages of the Self-Appraisal Question

More likely to be correct. Without doubt, one of the primary advantages of the self-appraisal question is that it takes away the tremendous burden of trying to interpret the meaning of the interviewee's comments. It really is not necessary to be a trained psychologist to understand and learn about how others behave. Interviewers who try to analyze the meaning of data during the interview often are misled and misguided by their own hunches and limited understanding of the complexity of the person in front of them. Let's look at it this way. Why settle for a second-order inference (your guess about what something means) when you have readily available a first-order inference (the applicant's analysis of what something means)? Strangely enough, given the right climate, most individuals have excellent ability to explain their behavior, even though they might not have been aware of this ability before the interview. In a sense, the interview can be a great opportunity for insights, not only for the interviewer, but for the applicant as well.

Helps avoid jumping to conclusions. Once the interviewer places the burden of interpretation on the applicant, then the temptation to assign meaning to data is sharply reduced, and the interviewer's mind is more open to explanations other than those he or she thought about. No longer is the interviewer likely to conclude that because someone graduated in the upper 10 percent of her class she is highly intelligent. But even more important, the self-appraisal question helps the interviewer to avoid jumping to gross, major conclusions because of a certain set or combination of facts. For example, suppose the interviewer is evaluating a candidate who is currently employed with a respected competitor. Assume further that during the interview it is learned the applicant is in a key management position, earning an excellent salary, especially for someone with his or her young age and limited work experience. In such an instance, it might easily be concluded that the candidate must be a good manager to have advanced that far so quickly. And, of course, such a conclusion is a logical probability. Notice what happens, however, when the self-appraisal question is introduced.

INTERVIEWER: Considering your few years with the company, you have really made excellent progress. Tell me [self-appraisal question], what would you say there is about you that may have accounted for your rapid progress at XYZ Company, and what, if anything, may have held you back from going even further?

APPLICANT: Well, I'm not really sure exactly what it might be, but I think I'm a fairly bright person. I pick things up rather quickly and I know when I was moved into several new departments, I was able to catch on very rapidly to what they were doing, so I got a lot of responsibility early on. And, I'll be quite frank with you, part of my progress was probably the result of my drive and ambition. I often talked with my supervisors about my progress and advancement, so maybe it was a little bit of my own push that helped. As far as what could have held me back, I can't think of anything serious. The only thing I can recall is that in my last performance review, my boss suggested there were times when I was a little too easygoing with my subordinates . . . but I don't think that was a critical thing.

At this point, it might be helpful to clarify the difference between the hypothesis method and the usual approach to evaluating data. In Figure 6, the *A* approach describes the typical reaction to a strongly positive bit of information; namely, the interviewer jumps to a conclusion (in this case, that the applicant must be a good manager to have advanced so rapidly). And, of course, this conclusion could be true or not true.

Now look at the *B* approach. Here the hypothesis method develops three hypotheses, making it difficult to jump to a totally erroneous conclusion about the applicant's strength as a manager. And, remember, the example cited here repre-

FIGURE 6.   Role of self-appraisal question in helping develop hypotheses.

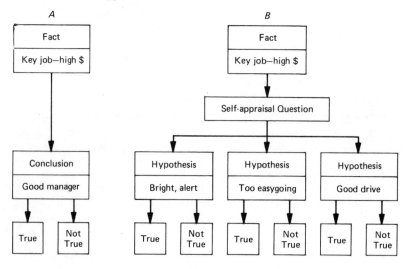

sents the hypotheses from only one self-appraisal question. Imagine how difficult it will be to prematurely conclude anything, if during the interview, many self-appraisal questions are asked so that forty to fifty hypotheses are generated.

Converts to predictable job behavior. A third, and perhaps the most meaningful, advantage of using the self-appraisal question is its help to the interviewer in converting the candidate's life history into predictable job behavior. This conversion can be readily noted in Figure 6. It can be readily observed how the fact about the applicants key job and high pay is translated into three significant hypotheses about how the individual might typically function. This is much more meaningful input for the interviewer than the conclusion that the candidate was a good manager.

Notice that even if the interviewer were correct about the good-manager conclusion (as shown in Part *A* of Figure 6), it would not necessarily mean that this particular candidate would be right for the interviewer's company. Perhaps the job for which he is being considered will require cleaning out a lot of deadwood. The fact that he might have been too easygoing with subordinates in his prior job could be a significant handicap in the new position. Or perhaps the opening for the candidate offers limited opportunity for advancement. Thus, while the applicant's ambition may have been helpful in XYZ Company, the same drive might soon result in dissatisfaction in his new assignment. The point is that it is essential to learn what lies behind the success he had with XYZ Company and to not be content merely with the information that the applicant advanced rapidly.

The historical facts or achievements in a person's background are really the "admission card" to the interview. If the facts are not good, it's not likely you will be interviewing the candidate in the first place. Once the applicant's background is reasonably acceptable, it's not so much more facts or achievements that are needed, but rather how or why the applicant accomplished them. Once an understanding is obtained about how the individual behaves and functions, then the interviewer has a sound basis for determining if the applicant can succeed in the job in question. It is the ease with which the self-appraisal helps convert historical data to on-the-job behavior that makes the hypothesis method so valuable for the interviewer.

Reduces chance of being fooled. A fourth advantage of the self-appraisal question is that it minimizes the likelihood of being fooled by articulate individuals or those experienced in interview-taking. Most applicants will not previously have been exposed to self-appraisal questions, which require candidates to think on their feet. Here is an example:

APPLICANT: [Mentions his family] Bill, my oldest brother, is an engineer, and Charles, my youngest brother, teaches phys ed in a local high school.

INTERVIEWER: [Asks the self-appraisal question] You and your brothers certainly took different career paths—you in sales, one brother in engineering, and the other in teaching. What differences do you suppose there are between your brothers and yourself that led them to go their ways and led you toward a completely different path?

In this case, the applicant now has to think out loud in order to answer. And as he responds, he begins talking about himself.

APPLICANT: I never really thought about it before, but Bill was always a much more studious person than I was. He had a real flair for math, and I guess I just enjoyed socializing more. I can remember him having a chemistry set and he loved to work down in the basement, while I would much rather be out with the fellows in the street playing ball or something . . . so I guess he went the science route. Now my brother Charlie, he's a little more like me. We both liked dramatics and, in fact, we were even in a few school plays together. I think he went into teaching because it gave him a chance to do a lot of different things . . . at least I think that's why he did it. As for me, when I got to college and took a look at the various subjects, I knew that marketing and sales would be right for me; I just like working with people.

As you can readily see, self-appraisal questions make it extremely difficult for the candidate to "snow" the interviewer. In order to do so, the applicant would have to first think of an answer to the question, decide that the answer would not be appropriate or not sound good, make up a new story, and tell it—doing almost all of these things simultaneously. And, even if the applicant were able to conjure a more favorable explanation than the truth, notice that what is said is recorded only as a hypothesis. For that hypothesis to become a confirmed hypothesis, the candidate would have to find occasion to lie or stretch the truth two or three more times during the interview—something that is extremely difficult to do.

To carry this thought further, it is important to realize that even though the applicant might lie consistently, other safeguards are available to the interviewer. As will be seen in Chapter 8 about recording data, as the confirmed hypotheses are studied, an incorrect one will become evident to the interviewer because, given all the other data available, it will not make sense. The inaccurate confirmed hypothesis that occasionally arises will probably not be given much weight or credence in the final hiring decision.

Self-appraisal questions are the interviewer's best defense against the polished and experienced interview-taker. Most applicants will not have thought through answers to the self-appraisal questions nor will they be able to gloss over falsehoods or inadequacies.

Self-appraisal questions are also helpful as good stimulators of conversation. Most people like to talk about themselves, and these questions definitely demonstrate the interviewer's interest in the candidate as a person.

Should self-appraisal questions be positive or negative in form? Interviewers rarely hear adverse information from a candidate when they ask direct questions. For example, the interviewer is at a distinct disadvantage when he or she asks a question such as, "How did you get along with your last boss?"

Applicants realize that the answer will be carefully considered, so they strive to give a response that makes them look reasonably prudent and that puts them in as positive a light as possible. Experience has shown, too, that negative characteristics are more likely to be mentioned during discussions in which applicants feel confident than during those in which they feel threatened.

Interview confidence can be engendered by a discussion in which applicants are encouraged to talk positively about themselves. The more statements applicants make about the good things they have done and accomplished and the good traits or characteristics they display, the more likely they will be to venture further and, perhaps even to their own surprise, reveal shortcomings about themselves.

It is recommended, therefore, that a majority of the self-appraisal questions—at the beginning portion of the interview, at least—be of the positive variety. Here are some typical examples of positive self-appraisal questions:

> "What good traits or qualities did you display that might account for your being elected president of your class?"

> "Are there any particular kinds of aptitudes you have that may account for your fine grades in the engineering curriculum?"

> "If I were to ask your high school coach what kind of a teammate you were, what do you suppose he would say?"

After the interviewer has asked three or four of these positive self-appraisal questions, most candidates will find it difficult to continually praise themselves. And having created such a favorable impression, they will then offer clues and direct statements about shortcomings. For example:

INTERVIEWER: What would you say it was about your personality that might have accounted for your being able to gain the cooperation of the older persons that you supervised?

APPLICANT: I guess I can explain that best by the fact that I'm a kind of even-tempered person. I didn't get upset very easily, and I didn't try to convey the idea I knew all the answers. Of course, I don't mean to convey the impression I never lost my temper or never sounded off. I guess we all do that a little bit, but most of the time I think I'm a pretty patient kind of guy.

INTERVIEWER: Well, we all get impatient with people from time to time. What kind of person or situation is likely to make you sound off?

Briefly then, it's probably better to keep the majority of questions on the positive side, although there is certainly no reason not to occasionally ask negative self-appraisal questions, particularly if the applicant has already mentioned a problem or difficulty. For example:

□ What is there about you that may have made that part of the job difficult for you?
□ In what ways would you need to grow stronger in order to be more effective at that?

Summary

The hypothesis method is a technique for assigning meaning to both observed behavior and historical data about the applicant's background. It is designed around the premise that the applicant's interpretation of the data is more likely to be correct than that of the interviewer. Use of the method requires that the interviewer ask self-appraisal questions, and then accept as hypothetically true whatever the applicant says in response to the self-appraisal question. If the same hypothesis emerges several times during the interview (thus confirming it), the hypothesis is accepted as being a true behavioral characteristic of the applicant. Of thirty to forty hypotheses generated during the interview, six to eight will usually be confirmed at the conclusion of the interview. For effective use of the hypothesis method, it is necessary to adopt an interview approach consonant with the emergence approach and the evaluation model (actual interview process) described in Chapter 9.

CHAPTER 8

How to Evaluate
What You Hear—
Recording the Data

At this point, it is probably obvious to the reader that it would be difficult, if not impossible, to remember all the hypotheses that are generated during an interview. For this reason, the use of the hypothesis method requires jotting down the hypotheses as they occur. To many, taking notes during an interview seems wrong, particularly in view of the need to keep anxiety and threat levels low. However, as shall be discussed here, the negative implications about note-taking are not as serious as they may seem. In fact, the reverse is usually true. Effective and efficient data gathering for employment interviewing invariably leads to note-taking.

Arguments Against Note-Taking

Those who believe that you shouldn't take notes usually state one or two reasons for their position. They will indicate that note-taking is threatening and, therefore, the quality and/or quantity of data obtained is reduced. Others object that note-taking is just too difficult for the average interviewer to manage during the interview. They point out that there are too many other things going on simultaneously—

asking questions, evaluating information, and observing behavior—and that note-taking becomes too much of a distraction. Let's examine both of these objections.

In my view, whether or not the taking of notes is threatening or anxiety-creating in the interview is a matter of how one takes notes. If the interviewer takes notes by having writing paper on top of the desk so that the applicant can peek over and see what is being written, this may prove distracting and possibly threatening. Or if the interviewer does not take notes consistently but only when the applicant says something negative, such action is likely to raise considerable anxiety or even alarm. But if neither of these procedures is followed, note-taking usually does not become a threat.

An effective way to take notes is for the interviewer to keep the notepad on the lap rather than on the desk. In this way, the interviewer can sit back in a chair and relax. If the interviewer's legs are crossed, usually the angle of the page is such that the applicant cannot see what is being written on the pad. The interviewer should make no attempt to hide the fact that notes are being taken but should angle the paper so that the applicant will not be distracted by seeing the writing on the page.

Another helpful note-taking procedure is to take notes fairly constantly during the course of the interview. When done steadily, the note-taking almost becomes a routine part of the scene. Because of its ongoing nature, the candidate may often become oblivious that notes are being taken. This is particularly true if the applicant is busy, doing most of the talking, and thinking aloud. An analogy can be drawn between interviewing and role playing with a video tape recorder. When the participants first begin the role play and face the camera, they are usually tense and uptight; as the role play proceeds, however, they become so involved in the task that they forget about the camera, and anxiety is reduced. The same is true for note-taking; as long as notes are taken steadily throughout the interview, the applicant's anxiety, if it exists at all, soon vanishes.

In contrast, the potential of an applicant being threatened or distracted by note-taking is clearly aggravated by the typical question-and-answer method of interviewing in which the applicant is not required to assume responsibility for carrying a significant portion of the interview. For example:

INTERVIEWER: Why did you decide to leave your last job?

APPLICANT: I didn't think the company gave me a chance to use most of my abilities.

INTERVIEWER: [Pauses to make notes about answer] I see, you wanted more chllenge and couldn't get it there?

APPLICANT: Well, it wasn't so much that, but. . . .

INTERVIEWER: [Pauses to make notes about answer]

Obviously, this kind of note-taking calls direct attention to the act of note-taking and is disruptive of a conversational style of interview.

If note-taking is at all threatening, the attendant anxiety can be significantly reduced by proper positioning of the notepad as well as by making the note-taking a consistent, ongoing process.

At this point, there may be some concern in the reader's mind about the ability to take notes on an ongoing basis. While this is an understandable concern, there is a solution. The solution rests, in part, with the interview procedures described in "Conducting the Evaluation Interview" (Chapter 9), and in the fact that the interviewer will not need to write down many words at one time. Usually, the notes will not consist of sentences or paragraphs but only one- or two-word descriptive phrases that emanate from the hypothesis method. The notes might read, for instance: *friendly, self-confident about abilities, highly aggressive, organizes thoughts well, tends to get lost in details.*

Before going further, the reader should be aware of recent research data about the impact of note-taking on the amount and depth of interview data obtained. In controlled situations in which persons were interviewed both with and without note-taking, no decrease in either the quality or quantity of data was found when notes were used. The results showed that those interviewers taking notes recalled (really had available) significantly more data than those who did not take notes. These findings were also corroborated by my own research. However, in one of these investigations, a high proportion of the population interviewed were from Western Europe—France, Germany, Belgium, and Holland. A slight, but not statistically significant, decrease in data was elicited by interviewers who took notes. It may be that similar problems could arise in note-taking with people of other cultures. In such cases, the interviewer must make a decision. Is the potential gain from note-taking worth the potential risk of less meaningful data being obtained? It is my practice to take notes, regardless of the cultural background of the candidate. I believe the gain far outweighs the potential loss.

Some interviewers object that it is too difficult to concentrate on asking questions, listening, guiding the interview, and taking notes at the same time. This is a problem if the interviewer burdens himself or herself with the mechanics of conducting the interview. Many interviewers, for example, are more concerned about what they are going to say next than in analyzing what is being said or in recording hypotheses. Fortunately there is a solution to this problem. It rests in conducting the interview in such a way that the burden of responsibility is on the applicant, so that conducting the interview requires little effort or attention. The model for conducting the evaluation interview, described in Chapter 9, provides just such an interview structure. If the interviewer follows the procedures of the model, there should be ample time to observe and study the applicant and also to develop and record the hypotheses.

Taking Notes after the Interview

Many interviewers, realizing the importance of remembering details, attempt to jot down recollections after the applicant has left. This procedure has three distinct disadvantages. It increases the time that the interviewer spends in the assessment task because it will take another ten or fifteen minutes to sum up the interview comments on paper, time that might better have been spent in the interview. Also, in most business environments, pressures of the day often make it impossible to write summary notes after completion of the interview—phones ring, secretaries come in with important questions, and meetings must be attended. These and other commitments frequently impinge on the interviewer, and the intent to do after-interview summarizing is frequently un-fulfilled.

Finally, there is the problem of differential recall. It is a well-documented psychological phenomenon that our mental set has much to do with what we recall. If, for example, the interviewer ends the interview with a generally favorable opinion of the applicant, then in recalling the findings of the interview the interviewer will remember more positive than negative factors about the candidate, even though the negative elements were observed. And if the impressions were not positive, the interviewer will differentially forget some of the positive aspects heard or observed and remember more negative ones. This phenomenon is often called the "halo-horns" effect. It obviously reduces the validity of prediction of job success.

Basically, there are few, if any, good reasons not to take notes; the alternatives are entirely unsatisfactory. Few professionals do not take notes when interviewing.

Note-Taking Techniques

There is no one best way to take or record notes. However, the approach used here, which I have developed, has been found to be highly satisfactory. A few ground rules will help clarify the process.

Do not use a printed or prepared form. Printed forms that have interview categories tend to focus the interviewer's attention on the printed items and questions rather than on the flow of conversation. If the interviewer feels the need for some format to guide him or her in the interview, broad categories such as "Education" and "Work Experiences" with ample blank space beneath each heading are the best approach.

Use a blank 8½″ × 11″ lined pad. Draw a line vertically down the center of the page. On one side of the page, record historical information and data about the applicant's background; on the other side of the page, record the hypotheses.

Relatively little should be written on the fact side of the paper since most of this kind of information is already recorded elsewhere—application blank, résumé, college transcripts, and so on. However, there will be instances when the interviewer solicits data that are not written elsewhere and that are important to remember. For example, as is shown in Figure 7, the interviewer may have asked why the applicant left college after his or her junior year; or, in another instance, what prompted the candidate to leave XYZ Company.

The bulk of the writing, however, should fall on the hypotheses side of the page. Here, as the reader may recall, the interviewer should record hypotheses from two basic sources. The first source is the observations the interviewer makes about the applicant's interview behavior—hypotheses

FIGURE 7.   *Example of interviewer's notes using Drake's method of note-taking.*

Facts	Hypotheses
coll – why leave jr. yr? father ill – needed $ help support fam not enjoy science courses left XYZ Company? wanted mgt work – recruited by agency	relaxed – seems self - confident communicates well impatient bright and articulate wants quick results for efforts verbally skillful not good at math drives self hard intolerant if not get own way can be "pushy" likes much variety and change in job enjoys people contact

such as *friendly, confident, detail-oriented, conceptualizes well, expresses thoughts clearly, appears disorganized, shows limited energy and drive,* or *personable.*

The second source of inputs for the hypotheses side of the page stems from the applicant's life history. These hypotheses are obtained by asking the applicant to self-appraise the hows and whys of the facts he or she presents.

During a typical assessment interview of an hour's duration, the interviewer is likely to accumulate three to four pages of notes, most of them one- or two-word hypotheses. When a hypothesis recurs, the interviewer can make a check mark next to the already written hypothesis. Figure 7 shows a typical page of facts and hypotheses.

The interviewer may also wish to make elaborative comments about some of the hypotheses. For example, the interviewer might ask the applicant why he was successful as a salesman, to which the applicant might respond, "Well, I rarely take no for an answer. I push hard and I'm quite aggressive in trying to close. I don't give up easily." Because the interviewer noted during the interview that the applicant was particularly forceful and quite aggressive in expressing his point of view, the interviewer might write next to his hypothesis, "rarely takes no—pushes hard" and the comment, "can see this." This represents another way to confirm or reject hypotheses.

Collating Hypotheses

Some professional interviewers can review their lists of hypotheses and mentally develop a pattern or a consensus impression of the overall balance of strengths and limitations. However, most interviewers cannot do this effectively without in some way organizing their thoughts. Perhaps the simplest way the interviewer can organize the list of hypotheses is to quickly examine the list and eliminate those for which there has been no additional support. It is difficult to pinpoint what represents adequate support in order to accept a hypothesis as being a true trait or characteristic. It is quite possible, for example, that the same hypothesis may appear only twice during the interview, but it is evident in such an obvious fashion, or with such strength, that it must be accepted as a true behavior characteristic. Other hypotheses may lack substance and definitiveness. The interviewer might like to see the trait, skill, or ability appear three or more times in the life history or in overt interview behavior before accepting it as true. This is a judgment that the interviewer must make.

The Balance Sheet

The end product of the evaluation process is a balance sheet of principal strengths and weaknesses. It is comprised of a listing of all the confirmed hypotheses. The interviewer must decide for each hypothesis whether it should be assigned as a strength or a limitation. Obviously, the correct placement depends upon a knowledge of the job. What is a strength for one job could easily be a limitation for another. As we shall see, however, this is not a problem for the interviewer to fret about. Regardless of in which column the hypothesis is entered, it is the interaction of the strengths and weaknesses that is important, not so much how accurately they are placed.

A typical balance sheet is shown in Figure 8.

Developing the balance sheet should not require much of the interviewer's time. It can usually be completed in less than five minutes at the conclusion of the interview.

Once the balance sheet is drawn, technique and methodology end; now the interviewer's judgment must prevail. When analyzing the balance between the strengths and limitations, the interviewer's knowledge of the job requirements and understanding of the elements of human personality and behavior are the ingredients that will help make a sound hire, not-hire decision. In essence, the interviewer's task is to weigh the strengths against the limitations and decide whether the resulting behavior pattern of this unique mixture of traits and abilities will enable the applicant to perform effectively in the job in question. As we shall learn later, the balance sheet is the tool used to begin the decision-making process. It will be compared against the job demands as described in the *behavioral specifications* (see Chapter 11).

Any interviewer following the hypothesis method will probably uncover more shortcomings than ever before. No longer will applicants be clearly seen as "good" or "not acceptable." Instead, the interviewer will list a large number of positive and negative characteristics. And, of course, this is realistic; each of us represents a constellation of strengths and limitations for any given job. Unfortunately, in many organizations, the objective of hiring "above-average candidates" translates to mean that the best applicant will have few, if any, identified weaknesses. It is almost universal that we tend to overreact to weaknesses. This is unfortunate because often the strongest candidate will manifest the most obvious shortcomings. For a fuller discussion of this point, see Chapter 11, "Matching the Candidate to the Job."

Evaluating Weaknesses

No one should be unduly prejudiced against a candidate simply because a significant number of shortcomings are confirmed and appear on the balance sheet. It is the specific

FIGURE 8.   *Balance sheet showing confirmed hypotheses.*

Strengths	Limitations
Quick thinker—bright and alert Energetic Likes contact with others and to be on the go Good drive—a self-starter Warm and personable Good insights about others Appropriate sales management experience	Impulsive—tends to act before thinking Basically soft—inclined to be too easygoing with others Seeks much credit and recognition for his efforts—likes to be in limelight

mix of strengths and limitations that is important; not the fact that shortcomings are evident.

A case in point appears on the balance sheet shown in Figure 8. Would the reader hire an individual with those qualities for an assignment, let us say, as regional sales manager? In this position the incumbent will be supervising other supervisors. When this question is asked in a classroom of business executives, the answer given is almost invariably no. The executives quite logically point out that such an individual might be too easygoing with subordinates; that customers might "get away with things" they shouldn't; that the manager might make false starts because of impulsiveness; and that he or she might not have a highly motivated workforce because of taking too much of the credit for subordinates' accomplishments.

All these conclusions seem reasonable, and yet this profile, somewhat simplified, was found to be characteristic of the most successful regional managers of a major food manufacturing company. In other words, the best regional managers in this particular company tend to have these qualities. Because the shortcomings are quite undesirable, how could these managers successfully direct large regions and still have such a configuration of strengths and limitations?

The experienced interviewer knows the answer lies in the extent to which the strengths offset the limitations. For instance, consider the shortcoming "Impulsive—tends to act before thinking." The regional manager may indeed be an action-oriented, decisive person who finds it difficult to sit back and plan for extended periods of time. But one of the positive characteristics possessed by this manager is that he or she is bright and alert. So while people may be action-oriented, it is not likely that their solutions to problems are going to be out in "left field." They are intelligent enough to develop reasonably satisfactory answers most of the time. They may not select the best possible answer, but they pick an acceptable answer. If they make a mistake, they may be quick and bright enough to notice the error before it goes too far. Moreover because they have "good insights about others," it is not likely they are going to make many serious mistakes in managing subordinates or customers. Imagine, on the other hand, if brightness and insight were absent. There are few executives more dangerous than those who are impulsive and stupid.

Another consideration when weighing the balance of strengths and limitations is the extent to which the shortcomings lend themselves to change or development. While some shortcomings may be serious, many can be ameliorated by coaching, experience, and maturity. We know, for example, that impulsiveness tends to lessen with age and maturity. We know, too, that even though a person may be basically soft underneath, he or she can learn to take a tough posture when it is necessary. It may be more difficult psychologically for the regional manager to make unpleasant personnel decisions, but he or she still makes them.

A third factor to be considered when evaluating shortcomings is the extent to which the shortcoming can be compensated for by the nature of the organization—that is, the degree to which the nature of the supervision, controls, policies, or structure of the organization reduces or eliminates the negative aspects of a shortcoming. For example, in the case of the regional manager described by the balance sheet, the company coped with the shortcomings by organizing the sales function so that each regional manager was teamed up with an analytical, financial-oriented partner. Together, as a team, the two of them ran the region. The company did not sacrifice the drive, enthusiasm, and marketing capabilities of the executive by trying to find more analytical or cautious candidates. Instead, the company reduced the risk of the weaknesses. In other cases, it might be recognized that the characteristics of the candidate's future supervisor will offset the shortcoming. For example, if one of the applicant's confirmed weaknesses is limited self-starting ability, such a shortcoming might not be serious if the applicant's strengths are good and if his or her boss is a hard-driving individual who will provide plenty of stimulation. Or the work environment may be highly motivating so there are enough built-in pressures that self-starting ability is not required for successful performance.

It is important, then, not to overreact to shortcomings as

such. Factors that are limitations for many jobs in a company might be assets in other jobs, depending upon the exact situation. In trying to determine the negative impact of any confirmed hypothesis appearing on the balance sheet, three analyses must be made: (1) the extent to which strengths offset or minimize each of the limitations; (2) the extent to which the shortcomings lend themselves to change or development; and (3) the extent to which organizational structure, supervisory personnel, or controls will compensate or offset the weakness.

Numerical Evaluation

It is strongly recommended that the interviewer, as he or she finishes an evaluation of strengths and limitations, assign a numerical rating to the candidate. Such a procedure takes less than a minute of the interviewer's time but yields some valuable assistance.

It helps to facilitate communication between several interviewers who see the same candidate. It also helps at a later date to distinguish among candidates, permitting the interviewer to readily place applicants in some sort of rank order.

Let us examine the numerical rating idea in more detail. The range of numbers assigned to the system seems to be of little significance, but the factors that are to be rated are important. A five-point rating scale is as follows:

1. Above average.
2. Average to above average.
3. Average.
4. Average to below average.
5. Below average.

It is possible, of course, to establish a nine-point or seven-point scale, but in practice the shorter scales seem to be quite sufficient.

A helpful way to use ratings is to base them on two factors: qualifications for the position in question, and potential for growth beyond this assignment.

Thus, at the end of the interview, the interviewer may

simply jot at the end of his page "Q–2, P–4." Such a notation indicates that this candidate is somewhat above average for the assignment in question but has limited potential to go beyond that point. On the other hand, a candidate might have a Q–4, P–2. That person is not particularly well qualified for the job but has sufficient underlying strengths that the interviewer believes the candidate can develop and over a period of time would have good potential to move further.

If interviewers were asked to list only a candidate's strengths and limitations, complete agreement on these factors might result, but different conclusions could be reached. Some assessors will focus on the candidate's long-range potential with the company, whereas others will center their evaluation on the candidate's ability to perform the job in question. Rating the candidate separately on each of the two characteristics helps to clarify each assessor's opinion of the applicant.

Assigning numerical values to candidates provides a second advantage in that it permits the interviewer to readily classify applicants at some future time. For example, if one interviews five candidates for a position during a week's time, it may become difficult to decide at the end of the week which candidate was best unless numerical values are designated. When numbers are assigned to candidates, it is easy to arrange them in rank order of preference.

Summary

To make effective use of the hypothesis method, note-taking is required to analyze and recollect all the hypotheses developed. While it is possible that note-taking during the interview could diminish the quality or quantity of data obtained, the advantages of note-taking, properly done, far outweigh any potential disadvantages. One should take notes consistently during the interview, using a lined pad with two sections, one for factual historical data and the other for the hypotheses. It was also suggested that the interviewer use the evaluation model for conducting the interview, so as to avoid a question-and-answer approach that calls undue attention to the note-taking.

Once the notes have been gathered and the interview is completed, it is recommended that the confirmed hypotheses be assembled into a balance sheet of principal strengths and weaknesses. To further clarify the interviewer's assessment, the assignment of a numerical rating, on the basis of qualifications for job and for growth potential, was also suggested.

CHAPTER 9

Conducting the Evaluation Interview

The point has now been reached when all the previously discussed segments of the interview can be integrated. This chapter provides a guide or model that explains exactly how the interviewer can proceed from opening comments to closing remarks.

The interview described here will be referred to as the evaluation interview. It is designed to provide sufficient information to enable the manager to make an informed, confident, hire, not-hire decision. At the conclusion of the evaluation interview, the interviewer should be able to produce a meaningful description of how the candidate will function on the job. In effect, this interview approach will help answer the question, "Will the applicant fit into our job?" An overview of this process is shown in Figure 9.

It should be understood that the evaluation interview is not a screening interview. Those are usually short interviews designed to weed out the unqualified on the basis of a limited number of essential requirements. The campus recruiting interview is an example of a typical screening interview.

The evaluation interview model described in this chapter allows the interviewer to use the emergence approach as well as the talk-generating techniques and hypothesis method in one easy-to-conduct procedure.

114

FIGURE 9. Model for conducting the evaluation interview.

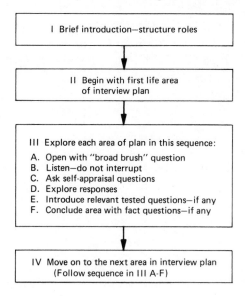

Structure Roles

Small talk should not be consciously emphasized when starting the interview. There is little reason for the interviewer to pospone obtaining meaningful input once the social amenities or introductory comments are completed. Instead of starting with obvious small talk about the weather or last week's football game, the interviewer can initiate the discussion with the first topic (life area) in his or her interview plan. For candidates with long work histories, it might be the life area of work experiences; for young, first-job hunters, high school would often be an appropriate place to begin.

It is also helpful at the outset to structure the interview so as to keep to a minimum interruption by the applicant. Interruptions often cause the interviewer to lose some control of the interview and make it difficult to maintain an easy, conversational discussion. To reduce the applicant's tendency to break into the discussion with questions about the job or the company, a statement that structures how the interview will proceed is helpful. Here is an example:

INTERVIEWER: In the time we have together here today, I know that we both want to get acquainted with one another. You want to be certain that our company is a good place for you, and we want to be certain that you're right for us. So let me spend the first portion of the time we have together getting acquainted with you, and then we'll turn it around and give you a chance to learn about us.

With this information, the candidate does not feel compelled to inerrupt the interviewer; he knows that eventually he will be given an opportunity to ask whatever questions he has on his mind.

Follow Interview Plan

In Chapter 3 the concept of a planned interview was introduced. As the reader will recall, such an interview helps ensure broad coverage of the candidate's life history and, hence, aids in obtaining information about each of the four fundamental sectors. The planned interview also provides two other advantages. It helps the interviewer maintain control, and it also makes the mechanics of conducting the interview easy. When the interviewer follows an outline of the nine major areas of exploration, he no longer has to worry about where he is going next in the interview.

One of the easiest ways to learn an interview plan is to list the preferred sequence of topics on a small card. By keeping the card on the desk the interviewer can refer to it from time to time during the interview. Once three or four interviews have been conducted with the same plan, the interviewer will no longer need to resort to the list.

The interviewer should consistently follow the plan and not skip about and should explore each area completely before moving on to the next one. When, for example, work experiences are being discussed, that entire segment of the applicant's life should be covered before moving on to some other life area such as leisure time.

Sometimes, however, the applicant makes only a brief statement about the area being discussed and then jumps to another area of the plan. When this occurs, the interviewer must interrupt the applicant and bring him or her back to the area under discussion. The following dialog illustrates one way of coping with this situation.

INTERVIEWER: Suppose you start by telling me a little bit about your high school days.

APPLICANT: Well, there is not too much to say. I went to Hackensack High School in New Jersey and then went on to the University of New Hampshire where I started my major in economics.

INTERVIEWER: I certainly want to hear about your career at New Hampshire, but before we get into college, let's go back and talk a little bit more about your high school days. What is there of interest that you can tell me about that period in your life?

Explore Each Area

When the interviewer begins to discuss an area, the conversation is controlled by asking the applicant questions that follow a specific sequence. The questions are arranged in such a way that it is unlikely the applicant will be aware that any particular model is being followed. More important, the sequence of questions lends itself to the development of hypotheses and helps keep the interview on a conversational plane. The pattern that is followed as each life area is explored is outlined in the following sections. The pattern is repeated over and over again as the various areas are discussed with the applicant.

Broad-Brush Questions

Each area starts off with a broad-brush question, that is, an open-ended question that does not indicate what specific information is sought. One of the best ways to frame a broad-brush question is to start with the invitation, "Tell me. . . ." A typical broad-brush question is, "Suppose you tell me something about your high school days."

This device is perhaps the single most important

technique for effectively conducting a conversational-style interview. Its great advantage is that it places the burden of responsibility for carrying the conversation directly on the applicant. With the "tell me" approach, it becomes quite clear to applicants that they are going to have to talk and to share themselves. Once the burden of responsibility is on the applicant, the interviewer is relieved of having to carry the conversation. The interviewer can almost adopt the role of a third party looking in on a discussion. It is this freedom from demanding responsibility that enables the interviewer to sit back, relax, and take notes—to make hypotheses about observed behavior.

Notice now, too, how many different hypotheses can be formed when the responsibility for determining what to say and how much to say is placed upon the applicant. Here are a few:

1. How well does the applicant communicate? Can the applicant express thoughts in a clear-cut, intelligible way or does he or she become tongue-tied? Are the applicant's vocabulary and communication skills adequate to the job in question?

2. How does the applicant think? Is the candidate able to conceptualize effectively or is thought superficial and shallow? Does the applicant organize thoughts in a logical, concise way or tend to ramble? Does he or she look at things from a broad perspective or become mired in detail?

3. The interviewer can also get some feel for the applicant's social perceptivity. If you ask an applicant to explain, for example, about his or her college career, isn't there a "right amount" to say? We don't expect the applicant to respond, by simply saying, for instance, that he or she "graduated in 1981." On the other hand, we don't expect the applicant to go on for half an hour telling about everything that happened each year, year after year. The applicant who has any social perceptivity will judge about how much should be said. The uncertain applicant may have sufficient social savoir-faire to ask how much detail is required. As experienced interviewers know, some applicants simply go on and on. The interviewer should let such applicants ramble at

length, for some time, in order to estimate just how poorly they judge (or misjudge) what is expected.

4. The broad-brush question also gives the interviewer the opportunity to get some feel for the applicant's ability to handle structure. Many applicants, upon hearing the broad-brush question, are likely to ask, "What do you want to know?" The interviewer should be prepared for such queries and be ready with a response such as, "I had nothing particular in mind; anything you'd like to share with me would be fine." Observing the applicant's struggle to handle the ambiguity of the broad-brush question provides valuable data to help the interviewer make hypotheses about the candidate's need for structure.

Another benefit of the broad-brush question is that it does not telegraph to the applicant what information is important to the interviewer. It makes it difficult for the applicant to pick and choose the "right" things to say. The candidate, in a sense, is given a blank slate on which to project and select those topics felt most impressive for the interviewer to hear. As a result, the interviewer will often learn about topics or situations he never thought about exploring.

An important advantage of the broad-brush question is that it provides the subject matter for the next step, the self-appraisal question. The response to the broad-brush questions is likely to be a paragraph or two about the candidate's achievements—the things that he or she believes will make a good impression on the interviewer. This is exactly what is desired. Discussion of the applicant's accomplishments keeps the interview atmosphere positive and nonthreatening. The applicant freely reveals information about self, thereby setting the stage for the how and why questions—the self-appraisal questions—that help the interviewer develop additional hypotheses.

Listen Without Interruption

Once the broad-brush question is asked, it is essential that the interviewer not interrupt the applicant's response. If the candidate's spontaneous response to the question is interrupted, it hinders evaluation of the candidate's ability to organize thoughts, to communicate effectively, and to be socially perceptive. In other words, the value of the broad-brush question is ruined when the interviewer interrupts the applicant's thought flow. This is particularly true if the interviewer interrupts with a question. At that moment, the responsibility of the interview will almost immediately shift back to the interviewer and then the interviewer will be forced to ask another question. Thus, the applicant now is in the role of passive-responder and the interviewer becomes the worker.

The no-interruption rule is difficult for most interviewers when first trying to learn the broad-brush questioning procedure. With so much data flowing out from the applicant, there is an almost overwhelming temptation to want to interrupt with questions to clarify or to find further information. If the interviewer feels compelled to say something, the listening can be done by using the acceptance techniques such as, "uh huh," "I see," "I understand," or even an occasional restatement—but no questions.

The only exception to this rule against interrupting is when the applicant directs the conversation away from the particular area that is being explored. Then it is necessary to intervene to keep the applicant on the topic. For example, the applicant may say something like this:

APPLICANT: I went to Kennebunk High School and graduated in 1980. Then I went on to the University of Maine where I majored in. . . .

INTERVIEWER: Excuse me, but before we go on the the University of Maine, let's just go back and talk a little bit more about high school. When we've finished that, we can go on and talk about college.

The way that the interviewer controls the interview is to keep the applicant locked in to the specific area being explored. Only when questioning sequence (broad-brush, self-appraisal, tested questions, fact questions) for the area is completed does the interviewer move on to the next area.

Ask Self-Appraisal Questions

Once the candidate has responded to the broad-brush question, the interviewer must begin developing hypotheses about the informaton that has been imparted. The manner in which the self-appraisal questions are used to develop hypotheses can be illustrated by the following dialog.

INTERVIEWER: [Broad-brush question] Suppose you tell me a little bit about your career in high school.

APPLICANT: Do you want me to talk about my grades or what?

INTERVIEWER: Oh, I had nothing particular in mind, just tell me anything that you think might be helpful for me to know.

APPLICANT: Well, let's see, I did fairly well in high school, as far as grades are concerned. I remember that I was on the honor roll four out of the eight terms. And I was pretty active in school. I played sports and had a varsity letter in soccer and track. I also had the lead in our senior play. I don't know what else to say. I enjoyed myself in high school; I had a lot of friends and took part in most of the social activities.

Once the applicant has concluded the response to the broad-brush question, the interviewer can begin asking self-appraisal questions about the achievements mentioned by the applicant. In this particular case, the accomplishments mentioned are as follows:

Good grades—honor roll.
Athletic achievement—team sports.
Lead in senior play.
Socially active.

The specific accomplishments the interviewer selects to inquire about depend upon judgment as to which of the applicant's comments will prove most productive for the development of hypotheses. Sometimes, only one of several statements will be queried; in other instances, almost everything the candidate reveals could be profitably explored. Here is how all four of the applicant's statements might be examined with self-appraisal questions, beginning with grades.

INTERVIEWER: [Self-appraisal question] You have indicated that you were on the honor roll four out of eight terms.

That's quite an accomplishment. What kinds of skills or abilities would you say that you have that might have accounted for those fine grades?

APPLICANT: I don't know really, but it seems that whenever I do anything, I like to do it right. I've always been that way; I guess that I was just very conscientious about grades. I've worked hard to get the good grades—I guess you'd just have to say that I applied myself well.

Possible hypotheses that could be written down from statements: *conscientious, sets high standards for self, accepts responsibility,* and *is hardworking.*

INTERVIEWER: [Self-appraisal question] You also indicated that you obtained varsity letters both in track and soccer. As you think back on it, is there anything you learned from your sports activities that you see carrying over as a help to you in adult life today?

APPLICANT: Well, yes, as a matter of fact, I did learn something from sports. I guess it was mostly from soccer. I never was a particularly good player, but I really liked the game and for the first two years I sat on the bench most of the time. It was pretty discouraging but I stuck with it and then in my senior year I made the first team and got my letter. I guess there were lots of times I thought about giving it up, but I stuck with it. I think what I learned from that experience is that if you really want to do anything just persist and you can accomplish it.

Possible hypotheses: *persistent, hard-driving,* and *tends to complete things he starts.*

INTERVIEWER: [Self-appraisal question] I notice you also mention that you had the male lead in your senior play. That's quite an honor. Tell me, what would you say your dramatic teacher saw in you that led him to pick you for the lead rather than someone else?

APPLICANT: Oh, I don't know. I was lucky I guess.

INTERVIEWER: [Restatement] It was only a matter of good luck.

APPLICANT: Well, no, I guess it wasn't only good luck. Like I said before, when I do something, I like to do it right. The night before rehearsal, I read over a section of the script and really practiced it. So when it came time for the try-outs, I went over pretty well. Most of the other fellows more or less read off the top of their heads, and I guess they didn't sound as good.

Possible hypotheses: *conscientious* and *needs to feel sure of self in new situations.*

INTERVIEWER: You also mentioned the fact that you were socially active in high school, had a lot of friends, enjoyed the dances, and so on. I assume you're telling me here that you got along well with most of the students.

APPLICANT: That's right. I had a lot of friends.

INTERVIEWER: [Self-appraisal question] Well, what would you say there is about yourself, say your personality, that might make it possible for you to get along so well with others?

APPLICANT: I don't know. I guess maybe it's my temperament. I don't think I get upset very easily, so a lot of people tend to confide in me. Maybe that's why people get along with me—I don't argue a lot with them.

Possible hypotheses: *even-tempered* and *tends to avoid conflict.*

Each of the examples should assist the reader in understanding exactly how the self-appraisal question helps translate the applicant's facts into behavior terms. The only difficult part of this process is the development of a wide variety of self-appraisal questions, so that the interviewer's actions do not become too obvious or repetitious. To aid the interviewer build a good repertoire of these kinds of questions, some prototypes are listed.

Prototypes for Self-Appraisal Questions

1. What skills do you have that might account for your fine success in _____ ?
2. Of course, not all things come easily to us. What was there about this particular __(job, course)__ that made it a bit difficult for you?

3. What was there about this __(class, job, hobby)__ that appealed to you? Why do you suppose you liked it? (This same question can be asked to elicit negative feelings by substituting "was unappealing" and "disliked.")

4. How would you evaluate yourself as a __(manager, fraternity president, salesperson)__? Good? Fair? Poor? What traits or skills do you have that might have accounted for your success?

5. If I were to call up your __(boss, teacher, coach)__ and ask him or her what kind of _____ you were, what do you suppose he or she would say?

6. You said that you were __(captain, president, chairperson)__. What do you suppose it was that your __(classmates, teammates)__ saw in you that led them to pick you rather than someone else?

7. You indicated that you were __(an only child, camp counselor, very poor)__. What impact would you say that experience has had upon your development as an adult?

8. You mentioned that you __(played team sports, were a "hot-line" counselor)__. What, if anything, would you say that you learned from that experience? What do you see carrying over to your adult life today?

9. You said that you have ambitions to become a __(district manager, nurse, company president)__. What is there about yourself that makes you think you would be a good _____? What area do you feel you might still need to develop before you could perform at an excellent level in that position?

The interviewer must make meaning out of the applicant's comments by asking the self-appraisal questions immediately after responses to broad-brush questions. It is important not to have other questions intervene between the conclusion of the response to the broad-brush and the beginning of the self-appraisal questions. If other questions are initiated before the self-appraisal questions begin, the interviewer will find it awkward to refer back later to those original points and difficult to make the interview flow smoothly.

When trying to develop hypotheses about the facts or

accomplishments presented in response to the broad-brush question, each accomplishment should be taken one at a time. It is helpful to make the bridge back to the original achievement or accomplishment by starting the self-appraisal question with the words, "You mentioned that. . . ." This bridging phrase helps the applicant focus on the topic under question and also gives the interviewer some time to formulate the working of the self-appraisal question. The questioning sequence is shown in Figure 10.

The interviewer should be aware that sometimes it is necessary to use additional questions as well as restatements and acceptances to draw out the applicant's response to the self-appraisal question. Sometimes applicants do not answer the self-appraisal question in a way that describes themselves and therefore the first answer must be followed up by additional probing and questioning. For example:

INTERVIEWER: [Self-appraisal question] You mentioned that you were a reporter on the school newspaper. Suppose I were to call up the editor of the newspaper and ask what

FIGURE 10. *Questioning sequence using self-appraisal technique.*

Interviewer's Activity	Interview Dialog
Open area with broad-brush question	INTERVIEWER: "Tell me about. . ."
Observe response and write down hypotheses about observed behavior	APPLICANT: (Describes accomplishments) "I did quite well at. . . . . .in my position at ABC." . . .in my position at DEF."
When applicant stops response to broad-brush, ask self-appraisal questions	
Record hypotheses as applicant describes how or why of each accomplishment	INTERVIEWER: "You mentioned that at ABC. . ." "You also indicated that at DEF. . ."

kind of reporter John Jones was. What do you suppose the editor would say?

APPLICANT: I don't know what he would say.

INTERVIEWER: Well, I know you wouldn't know what he would say but you could probably speculate on what he might say. What would you guess he would say?

APPLICANT: Well, he would probably say I always got my story. [Notice in this example that the answer does not tell us anything directly about the applicant. The fact that he "always got his story" really doesn't tell us anything about how the person functions or behaves. Thus, some additional probing is necessary.]

INTERVIEWER: Can you elaborate on tht a little bit? What does that really mean?

APPLICANT: Well, it often was necessary to interview someone to get the story, and some of these people were difficult to reach, like the mayor of the town or the president of the university.

INTERVIEWER: Well, how could you do that? What did you do that made that possible? [Notice, again, the self-appraisal to learn how or why he accomplished this.]

APPLICANT: Well, you see, I wouldn't give up on them. I'd try to reach them at the office; if they wouldn't talk with me on the phone, I would wait outside their office until they came out after work and try to catch them then. If they would not talk to me then, I would wait until that night and call them up at home. If that didn't work, I'd try to catch them as they came out of the house in the morning and went to their car in the driveway. I would just wear them down and sooner or later they'd say, "Okay, I'll give you the story." I guess they used to give me the story just to get me off their backs.

As the reader can note, it took a number of questions before it was possible to extract behaviorial meaning from the applicant's work as a school reporter. In this case, we probably would have written a hypothesis such as *persistent.* Some of you may have interpreted it as *pain in the neck.* In any case, the hypothesis finally arrived at is far more helpful than the fact that the person "always got his story."

Introduce Relevant Tested Questions—If Any

When all the self-appraisal questions for the respective area have been asked, the interviewer can introduce the tested questions that are appropriate to the area being discussed. Each interviewer should have, at the tip of his tongue, a few questions to weave into the interview plan. For example, when talking about college, always ask the applicant why he selected the college he attended and why he chose a particular major subject. As the applicant responds to these questions, the interviewer, of course, can develop and record additional hypotheses.

If the reader has done substantial interviewing, he will probably already have developed his own repertoire of tested questions. If the reader is relatively inexperienced at interviewing, then it would be worthwhile to learn one or two tested questions for each of the interview areas.

Appendix A lists approximately 100 tested questions that could be added to the interviewer's repertoire. These tested questions are listed by life area and also indicate the likely hypothesis that each question will yield. This list can be especially helpful if the interviewer is experiencing some difficulty in obtaining sufficient data about one of the four basic factors (intellect, motivation, knowledge, personality). You should select tested questions that will produce more hypotheses in the area in which you seek more data.

Conclude Area with Fact Questions—If Any

Fact questions are inquiries about events in the applicant's life history. For example, the candidate's application blank may have indicated that he or she received a scholarship to college. The interviewer may want to know the basis upon which that scholarship was awarded—whether it was for scholastic achievement, athletics, financial need, or whatever.

Most fact questions usually will be asked about work experiences. Specific questions about how things were done on the job, what was done, the approaches taken, and the specific skills learned or needed are quite appropriate. Educational background is another area about which many fact questions will probably be asked.

In other life areas, however, fact questions are often not required. For instance, in discussing the person's leisure-time activities, or goals and ambitions, few fact questions are necessary. The emphasis in these areas should be on questions that emanate from the applicant's response to the opening broad-brush question.

Move on to Next Area in Interview Plan

When the interviewer has completed the exploration of an area, he is ready to move on to the next area in the plan. Because he or she knows exactly what that topic will be, the transition from one area to the next is made smoothly as part of the ongoing conversation. When the interviewer enters the next area, he once again begins with the broad-brush opening question and repeats the step-by-step procedures described in the evaluation model.

While the model may appear somewhat mechanistic and structured to the interviewer, the applicant will rarely be aware that any plan is being followed. Moreover, the interviewer is in complete control throughout the process, knows where he or she is at each point in time, and has a firm hand on the pace and course of the interview. For the applicant, the interview will appear as a generally pleasant conversation with a gentle sense of direction.

Most candidates will like this approach to interviewing because it is so applicant-centered. Many will indicate, "This is the first time I have really been interviewed." What they are saying is that this is the first time anybody tried to understand who they were—tried to understand them as a person, rather than as a technician, engineer, supervisor, or whatever. Interviewers are concerned that the applicant has the necessary background qualifications to perform effectively, but what makes this type of interview so different is that there is considerable focus on how the person behaves on the job and the reasons behind that behavior. Most candidates find it enjoyable to talk about themselves, once it is understood that the interviewer is eager to hear details about the person's life. Even the most shy applicant will often open up freely when the interviewer seems interested in him or her as a person.

Many companies indicate that this approach is one of their best recruiting devices, because it so distinguishes their interviews from those of other organizations.

Concluding the Interview

Most interviewers who follow the model described in this chapter will require forty-five minutes to an hour to complete the interview. At times, the interview may take longer if there is extensive work history to explore. Unless the candidate is obviously unqualified, the interview should not be terminated in less than twenty minutes—even if the applicant seems weak. Often strengths that do not appear at the outset of the interview manifest themselves later as the candidate relaxes and communicates more freely.

Terminating the Discussion

A good strategy for concluding the interview is to let the applicant close it. This can be accomplished by one of two easy steps. The interviewer can nonverbally signal that the interview is over by placing his notepad and pencil down on the desk. Or the interviewer can say, "I think we've discussed all that we need to cover for now. Is there anything else that you would like to add?"

The applicant will usually respond in either of two ways to the statement. He may say, "No, I can't think of anything else," in which case the interview is over. Or the candidate may say, "You never asked me about the summer jobs I had. In two of them I had some very good experience in cost estimating, so perhaps I should tell you about some of the projects I was involved in."

In the second instance, the interviewer should encourage the applicant to say what he wants about the summer work and then ask, "Is there anything else you can think of?" At this point, the applicant is likely to say no, and the interview can be terminated.

This strategy is also quite effective when the interviewer

desires to terminate the interview before it seems appropriate to the applicant.

In most instances, no additional techniques are needed to conclude the interview. What makes the method described so satisfactory is that the applicant is given the chance to say whatever is on his mind. In effect, we are letting the applicant end the interview whenever he or she decides nothing further can be added. It is also helpful if the interviewer strives to select, for the last topic in the interview plan, a subject that is relatively easy to talk about. One life area that is quite appropriate for closing is leisure-time activities.

When an offer of employment is not going to be extended, it is usually best to indicate to the applicant that you are considering several other candidates before you make your final decision. Say that as soon as a decision is reached you will let him or her know. Except in the obvious situation in which the candidate knows that he or she is not suited to the job, the interviewer should not tell the candidate on the spot that he or she is unacceptable. If the interviewer follows such a procedure, he may open the door to an endless haggle or defense of the candidate's rejection. It is also possible, once the other candidates have been interviewed, that the interviewer might want to reopen the discussion with a questionable candidate. Telling the candidate that you will be in touch soon is usually a gentler way of letting a person down and also a more efficient way of handling the end of the discussion.

Selling the Company and the Job

The selling of the applicant on the job or the company really begins at the outset of the interview—not explicitly, of course, but merely by the manner in which the interviewer conducts the discussion. Candidates are often positively influenced by the degree of sincere interest the interviewer shows in them. The formal sell should be initiated only after the interviewer has decided that the candidate is acceptable. There is little value either in trying to simultaneously evaluate and sell or in first selling and then assessing. If the applicant is unacceptable, both of these approaches waste time. Of course, a certain amount of selling is good public relations, regardless of how the interviewer feels about the applicant.

The sales portion of the interview can be divided into two distinct phases: the applicant's questions and inputs from the interviewer about the job and company.

Applicant's questions. An excellent way to begin influencing the desired applicant toward accepting a company offer is to solicit questions from him or her. These questions usually reveal the applicant's areas of concern or interest and should receive considerable attention from the interviewer. Each question provides a platform from which the interviewer can relate how the company can meet the candidate's needs and interests. The most effective type of question is the open-ended one such as, "What is there that you would like to know about us?" or, "Are there any problems or concerns you have, at this point, about the company, the people, or the job?"

Interviewer's input. Once the applicant's questions have been answered, the interviewer can provide additional information to help the candidate make a decision about the company. The most helpful comments are usually those that review job responsibilities, growth opportunities, and company style or philosophies.

Detailed information and suggestions for selling your organization to the job candidate are outlined in Chapter 10, "Selling the Candidate—Managing the Visit."

Additional Points about Conduct of the Model

To make effective use of the hypothesis method, it is necessary that the interviewer explore a wide range of topics about the applicant's background. The depth, however, to which each area is probed will vary according to the interviewer's judgment about two factors—the number of hypotheses that can be generated from discussion of the area and the relevancy of the area to job success.

Depth of Exploration

It is recommended that every area of the interview plan be explored. This procedure is often called "dipping in." It is important to follow such a process because failure to do so may result in significant information being missed. Even for such seemingly irrelevant areas as early family life, the interviewer has no way of knowing what potentially fruitful hypotheses could be developed from such a discussion unless he or she inquires about the topic.

When the response to the opening broad-brush question seems to reveal little data upon which hypotheses can be built, the interviewer can simply go on to the next area. It is important, however, to develop as many hypotheses as possible per minute of time. A good rule of thumb for the interviewer is to ask at least one self-appraisal question in each area.

The second factor that determines the extent to which a given area will be explored is the relevancy of the area; that is, the area's proximity in time to the job in question. Most of the interviewer's time—65 percent or so—should be devoted to discussion of relatively current life history such as recent work experience and education, leaving 35 percent of the time for discussion of more remote areas such as early childhood, high school, and the like.

Use of Résumé or Application Blank

It is not recommended that résumés or application blanks be used by the interviewer during the interview. These props make it difficult to keep the interview conversational and often lead the interviewer astray. If the interviewer follows the content of a résumé or application blank, there is a strong tendency to focus on what is recorded there and to assume that is the whole story. Obviously, many things happen in people's lives that never appear on an application blank. What is written there is only what the applicant wants you to see.

There is also a tendency, while following a résumé or application blank, to assign a certain motivational logic to the candidate's activities. The reason for this is that most application blanks are arranged in a logical, sequential fashion.

Thus, by reviewing the application blank, it would appear an activity at one stage of the person's life led to a subsequent one. However, life rarely goes along in such a logical, organized manner. There are jigs and jags and often unexplained and unmentioned time gaps. Thus, the interview tends to gloss over segments of the applicant's life that would have been pursued in greater depth if the interviewer were not using the application blank as a springboard for the interview discussion.

Following a printed page also makes understanding the applicant more difficult. The interviewer should always try to understand the reasons for the sequence of events and changes in the applicant's life. To accomplish this, it is often helpful for the interviewer to ask, "And then what happened?" If the résumé is directly in front of the interviewer, it is rather awkward to raise such questions.

Candidates will often offer the interviewer a résumé or application blank at the outset of the interview. At such times it is best to look at the historical background rather briefly—noting any red flags or possible trouble spots. Then the interviewer can gracefully put it aside by saying, "Thank you very much. I'll look it over carefully later, but now I would like to hear the story from you."

One great value of the planned interview, with its prescribed areas to explore, is that it makes the conduct of the interview relatively easy for the interviewer. Little energy should be expended in coping with the mechanics of the interview; instead, effort should be directed toward the development of the self-appraisal questions and the recording of the hypotheses.

Summary

The model for the evaluation interview provides a guide for conducting a hire, not-hire interview—from the introductory remarks to the terminating comments. Small talk is not recommended to begin the interview, but the interviewer should structure the roles in the interview by advising that the applicant will have an opportunity to ask questions later.

The interviewer should consistently follow the plan and explore each area completely before moving on to the next one. Start the discussion of each area with a broad-brush question and listen without interruption to the applicant's response. Once the candidate has replied, ask self-appraisal questions and then any tested questions that are appropriate to the area being discussed. Conclude with fact questions if any are necessary and move on to the next area in the plan. To terminate the discussion, signal the interview is over by a nonverbal sign such as placing the notepad on the desk or by asking if the applicant has anything to add. The sales portion of the interview logically follows the assessment of the candidate.

CHAPTER 10

Selling the Candidate—
Managing the Visit

There is nothing more frustrating (and costly) than having recruited and evaluated an excellent candidate only to have that applicant turn down the job offer so that the whole process has to be started over again. Effectively marketing the company and the job is as important a part of the selection procedure as recruiting or evaluating. Unfortunately, an organization often gives scant attention to determining that the applicant it wants also wants it. This assumes that if a company offers employment, a person will accept it. A company that seeks the most desirable individuals, those who other organizations also want, must remember that the candidate is evaluating it just as it evaluates him or her.

This chapter describes an effective procedure for attracting candidates, particularly to job situations or locations that might not be considered highly attractive or desirable. What is desirable varies from person to person but, typically, remote plant locations, harsh climates, and large cities (even though glamorous to some) may be viewed by many as undesirable, despite good pay and benefits. Sometimes an organization attracts candidates because of its preeminence in the industry or because it is situated in a highly desirable location. Even so, for the most sought-after candidates, a company must pay attention to the sales aspect of the employment process. The procedure described here has been effective for many organizations and is particularly helpful when the geographical location may not be highly attractive to the applicant. In the description of the procedure, the word *plant* is used frequently. However, if your organization is located in an office in a city, the recommendations are equally appropriate.

Some Basic Assumptions

Before we depict a selling approach, let us make some basic assumptions. First, we will assume that the candidate has passed some initial screening or filtering. The candidate may have been recruited by an executive search firm, interviewed by the personnel department, been recruited on campus, or sent to headquarters for approval following assessment by a regional office. The assumption is that the company would like to attract this candidate who seems well suited to the job. The procedure, of course, provides ample opportunity for conducting the evaluation interview that was discussed in Chapter 9, so there remains the possibility that the candidate may be eliminated after the sales visit. Let us also assume that the compensation and benefits are competitive, that there is a career path—a place to grow—for new employees, and that the organization is reasonably successful.

In examining this approach for increasing the acceptance rate of the best candidates, it must be recognized that many things need to be "sold" to the candidate, aside from the job. We need to sell the company, the location, and most important, ourselves. All these factors enter into the candidate's decision whether or not to join an organization, and all should be adressed in any effort to recruit the new employee. The premise on which this procedure is built is that familiarity is the best antidote to resistance to something new or different; that "hands-on" exposure to job, potential co-workers, and community environment are all important in helping the applicant overcome possible objections to accepting the employment offer. Ultimately, the probability of positive reaction to the offer depends upon the candidate's ability to identify with the employment situation—to see himself or herself happily engaged in the life-style of that company and the community environment.

Essential Ingredients in Winning Top People

Involve all key managers. The visit to the location should not involve only the personnel department and the candidate's future boss. All individuals with whom the applicant is likely to interface, once on the job, should be briefed on the candidate's background before the visit. When the applicant is being shown around the facility, the key employees he or she meets should not be caught unawares. They should know enough about the candidate to provide a warm welcome and to make constructive comments as positive support of the recruiting effort. This briefing of key people can be made during a staff meeting when the group is together for other purposes. At that time, the candidate's background should be reviewed and discussed and agreement reached on which aspects of the operation would be meaningful and could be highlighted during even casual discussions.

Organize team operation. The on-site visit should be a carefully structured team operation—team in the sense that many individuals will be involved, including frequently the spouses of some of the executives. Specific assignments should be delegated to various members of the executive group.

Allow adequate time. It is not cost-effective to bring an important candidate for an on-site visit and whisk him or her through many interviews, a quick lunch, and then off to the airport. It is my experience that thirty-six hours is not too much time from arrival to departure; twenty-four hours should be considered minimal. To have a candidate successfully identify with the operation, the individual needs firsthand exposure to the activities at the site. One needs to see how a company operates, how one would fit in, be accepted, and the like. The applicant also needs time to view the nonjob aspects of the position (community, schools, housing) and to digest what was discussed and seen during the

first day of his or her visit. Therefore, periods of time overnight, when the candidate and spouse can discuss and reflect
on these issues and prepare questions for the following day,
are vitally important.

Involve candidate's spouse. In this age of dual careers, emphasis on quality of life issues, and concern about family
stability, it is inexcusable not to involve the candidate's
spouse (if one exists). Usually the spouse will be a significant
factor in the longevity of the candidate's stay with a company.
If upon relocation the spouse finds work opportunities limited, or the children unhappy, or the community lacking in
satisfying experiences, the likelihood of the candidate staying
with the organization is, of course, greatly reduced. It makes
good sense to involve the candidate's spouse when trying to
gain commitment from a top candidate.

Designate host and hostess. One of the key assignments is
that of an executive and spouse to act as host and hostess so
that the candidate is treated as an honored guest and not
simply a job applicant. The host and hostess might be the
candidate's future boss and spouse or a more senior executive and spouse. In any case, the host and hostess should not
be slotted lower in the organization hierarchy than the level
at which the candidate will be placed. If the key person the
company is attempting to sell will come in as the president or
top official in the location, it may not be practical for a head-
quarter's couple from outside the location to serve as host
and hostess. The host and hostess should then be selected
from among those who are actively involved in the community, are warm and friendly individuals, and are well respected in the organization.

Provide on-the-job contacts. An effort should be made to
involve the candidate with people he or she can identify with,
that is, individuals of similar age, job function, and life-style.
Candidates want to know what people like themselves are
doing, how they live, and how they function. Making available persons with whom the applicant can relate and talk is
analogous to sending a recent graduate from a particular
university back to that campus to recruit graduating seniors.
The young students can readily identify with this individual,

so the interviewer often has more success than a senior manager.

Involve the prospective boss. If executives in your organization are going to be held accountable for their productivity, then they should be directly involved in making the decision about who should be working for them. For this reason, and because "chemistry" between individuals is an important ingredient in successful work relationships, the prospective boss of the candidate should be directly involved in the interview process, the final decision, and the job offer. Often, it is this individual who actually extends the final offer. There is no reason to wait until the first day the candidate reports to work to start building this relationship. It should begin at the time of selling the candidate.

Offer real-life activities. An effective way of selling candidates is to let them get a feel for what it would really be like to work in the organization. This cannot be gained by verbal descriptions of "how we operate here" or telling the person that it is a "good place to work." It is important for the candidate to experience something more concrete, more tangible. An example of this approach can be seen in a study I did for a client organization. For this company, fifty-six college seniors were asked why they accepted the company's offer of employment. Of that group, thirty-three, or 57 percent, indicated "clear image of job assignment" was the primary reason for accepting the offer. In effect, they were saying that when they got their offering letter they could visually depict the job they were going into; it was concrete, not some vague abstraction.

In this company's selection process, the evaluation interviews were conducted in the morning. During the afternoon, the candidate was assigned to an individual who was new in a job similar to that the candidate would fill. The candidate was allowed to "tag along" with the employee as daily job responsibilities were carried out—writing reports, answering the telephone, attending staff meetings, and so on. Thus, by the end of the afternoon, the candidate had a real feel for what the job would entail, and the nature of the work environment, and even a sense of identification with the organization. Many candidates said that during the afternoon they felt as though they were already "on board."

In essence, it is important to involve the candidate in real-life, day-to-day activities at the location. These could include morning production planning meetings, project review conferences, and the like.

Deal with hidden needs. To be effective in selling key people, it is important to consider hidden needs as well as those customarily expressed. As you talk with candidates, the expressed needs will be explicit questions about the challenge of the work, the nature of future opportunities, and the compensation and benefits. Obviously, the organization should be prepared to answer these clearly and definitively. But there are also hidden needs that affect the candidate's decision. These needs are sometimes not raised because the candidate fears they may be interpreted as signs of insecurity or weakness. Following are a few hidden needs that any effective selling program should consider.

Working atmosphere. The candidate needs a chance to see the whole business picture to provide a sense of completeness and understanding of what makes this organization tick. At a more subtle level, most candidates are trying to determine for themselves, "Is this a stimulating kind of environment? What are the possibilities for my personal growth and involvement in the organization?" Most candidates want to know, for example, the true extent to which they will participate in goal setting or have autonomy in their job. Candidates may fear they will find the environment stifling or will be narrowly boxed into a small segment of the business. They worry about whether or not they will be cut off from the mainstream or have much control over their own environment, work flow, or decisions. The degree to which the company can deal with these hidden concerns, which center about the person's ability to be a meaningful part of the organization, will in large measure determine the probability of acceptance of the offer.

Life-style. Many organizations focus so much on the job and the organization that they fail to address the concerns candidates may have about what it's like to live in the particular area or community. The candidate does not always express a question of real concern, "Is this a place that I want to live and raise my family in?" Essentially, the candidate's concerns are about opportunities for off-the-job activities, association with people of like interests, the quality of the schools, the opportunity for the person's own personal growth, and opportunities for family recreational activities.

The more positive answers are supplied to these questions, the less concern the job candidate will have. It is not good enough to merely link the candidate up with a real estate agent and hope that the trips around town will satisfy the concerns and needs. Perhaps the most critical question on the list just mentioned is association with people of like interests. The candidate and his family naturally wonder how they are going to fit into the community in much the same way that a job candidate wonders about fitting into the organization. It's important, therefore, to show the candidate what a community offers to make life satisfying. This usually requires during the interview a direct question about what is important to the person and the family life-style. It might be helpful to ask what the candidate's family enjoys where they currently live, so that information can be gathered on opportunities in the local community that might satisfy these same interests.

Bridge from present life to new one. This really has to do with such questions as, "What will it be like living here?" and "Will I succeed?" It has much to do with who the candidate and his or her spouse meet during the visit and the extent to which they see these people as welcoming them into the company and community. This may mean that some of the people doing the interviewing and meeting with the candidate should share some of their activities and life-style. They should be instructed to be genuine, sharing some of the negatives as well as the positives. Without being obvious about it, those involved in the selling visit should be prepared to provide answers to the questions mentioned in this section.

An Effective Format for Visiting Candidates

This section presents a list of suggested activities for a two-day visit. In this example, let us assume that the candidate is a male and his wife is the spouse. If the situation is reversed, or if the candidate's wife is employed, some revisions in the suggested schedule must be made to allow time for the candidate's spouse to explore employment opportunities. In such cases, it would be helpful if the personnel department worked directly with the spouse, describing employment opportunities in the area, salary levels, and major industries. The personnel manager might also be requested to line up interviews with local executive search organizations, employment agencies, and personnel departments in the area. Short of that, supplying brochures from the major employers in the area would be desirable.

The procedure outlined here has been tested and has worked effectively with a large number of candidates but, obviously, represents only one of many ways of making a visit effective. Local situations also may require adaptations.

Before Arrival of Candidate

Mr. and Mrs. Candidate should be contacted well before their arrival by the assigned host and hostess. They should know where they are going to stay, who will meet their plane, and what they will be doing. This can be done by letter, but it is often best to combine written communication with an informal telephone conversation to learn if the candidate has any questions about the visit. There may be, for example, some questions about the climate and appropriate clothing to pack.

Arrival

If possible, it is desirable to have the candidate and spouse arrive the evening before the first full day. The host and hostess should meet the plane, conduct the guests to the hotel or motel, and at that time explain the next day's activities. Essentially, it will be a busy day at the plant or office for the candidate, a relaxed day around town or visiting employment possibilities for the spouse, and dinner with company host and hostess for both.

It is also helpful, before leaving the guests on the arrival evening, to give them a packet of information regarding the community and the company. These could be Chamber of Commerce maps, brochures describing local places of interest, company benefit package outlines, annual reports, and company house organs or magazines. The meeting the first evening should not be long. The travelers may be tired, and so, after explaining briefly what will happen the next day and what time they will be picked up, let the guests retire.

Next Day; Wife's Program

The hostess picks up the candidate's wife at about 9:30 A.M. and spends the morning showing her a few community points of interest, including schools. The hostess arranges lunch with two (maximum of three) carefully chosen hostesses.

The hostess offers to turn the visitor over to a local cooperating realtor for a couple of hours during the afternoon. She also arranges for the wife's return to the motel at 4:30 to freshen up and rest before a happy hour at 6 P.M. to be followed by dinner.

Next Day; Candidate's Program

The following is a typical first-day schedule.

8 A.M.—Plant (or location) briefing. This should be kept short, no more than twenty minutes. It would be helpful to use an expert for this who is skillful in presentations, perhaps someone in the training department. The briefing might include slides or a film, including maps and exhibits to brief the applicant on the nature of the operation, what is done, and how it is accomplished. In effect, this gives the person a good overview of what the place is all about.

8:30 A.M.—Plant or location tour with future associate. In this portion of the day, the applicant is assigned to someone who is in the same type of job as he will be filling. The candidate is given the opportunity to follow this employee around as he goes about his morning chores. It would be helpful if they could drop in on morning meetings, such as a project review meeting, a production or maintenance planning meeting, or perhaps the plant manager's staff meeting. These should be ongoing meetings conducted in the usual way, whether a candidate is there or not. If the employees are preparing a report, they might involve the candidate in this process.

11 A.M.—Candidate visits his future department and is introduced to other associates in the operation. A round-table discussion may focus on the objectives of that particular department, the problems it is currently facing, some of the hopes for solving them, and how they and the potential incumbent might work together. Some description of how the department functions as a team should be included.

12 noon—an informal lunch during which the respective groups discuss goals, views of the organization, and the business or industry. Again, this is a shop talk kind of meeting where the candidate gets a chance to see who he will be interfacing with, how they view his department, and how they probably will be working together in the future.

1:30 P.M.—Interview with the manager and future boss. In this time segment the manager should use the evaluation model discussed in Chapter 9. It should be a serious attempt to make a sound, qualitative assessment of the candidate. After completion of the assessment portion of the interview (completion of the evaluation model), the manager will explore the candidate's reactions and perceptions. Open-ended questions should be asked as to what the candidate's reactions are thus far, what he sees as some of the positive aspects of being in the organization, and any concerns the applicant may have. In addition, the manager might invite comments on how the candidate would like to contribute to the organization. This is a good opportunity for the manager to practice listening skills. Finally, the manager might end the meeting with a review of the total picture. Some topics that may be touched upon are:

1. Business strategy of the organization and its competitive position.
2. The management style of the organization and how the manager likes to operate.
3. Investment planning.
4. Objectives for the future.

The purpose is to bring the candidate into the "fold" by really giving him a feel of what the company is about, where it's going, and how it is managed.

3:15 P.M.—Session with personnel manager. Here the candidate is exposed to the company policies, benefits, and information about where the personnel in the organization are living, the schools, and so forth. It also provides a time to inquire how the candidate feels about the company. The candidate also should be invited to ask any questions he has about the company or the community.

4 P.M.—Return guest to motel. The company representatives who have been seeing the candidate can now get together to share views on the suitability of the applicant and next steps in the selling process. Usually this includes the manager, the host, tour guides, and the personnel representative. At this discussion, it would be well to evaluate the candidate by comparing numerical ratings on qualifications, potential, and any concerns that anyone has. At this time, it can also be decided who will explore any questionable areas and how this will be fed back to the decision maker (the manager). This new information will usually be gathered that evening or during the following morning.

6 to 6:30 P.M.—Happy half-hour.

6:30 to 8:30 P.M.—Dinner with manager (if seriously interested), wife, host, and others. A party of six is recommended, but never more than eight. The brief period keeps drinking moderate and adjournment early. There does not seem to be any great advantage in "doing the town" or making this a lavish affair. Dinner in a quiet, good restaurant with an opportunity to talk in a relaxed manner is probably the best.

During the dinner, which should be on a pleasant social level, questions from the candidate and spouse can be answered, but no explicit attempt is made by the company staff to probe or question at this time.

If the organization is still feeling quite good about the candidate, positive comments (not a job offer) should be made during the dinner simply to show favorable disposition. It would be well if the candidate and his spouse could retire that evening having positive feelings about the organization and also feeling optimistic about employment possibilities.

Second Morning

The second morning is when efforts are made to "close the deal." And this is when the manager should play the major role. It would be helpful if three major points were made.

We like you. Indicate that all who have met the candidate feel that he would be an excellent member of the team, that he's the kind of person who would fit in well. It could be mentioned further that all foresee a working relationship that would be cooperative and enjoyable.

We need you. Point out that the offering is a critical job that really needs to get done, and that the applicant is believed capable of accomplishing it.

You will succeed. Point out, in an optimistic way, that you believe the candidate could make an excellent contribution. Indicate confidence that the candidate will find much satisfaction in completing what needs to be accomplished.

If terms of the job offer have not been put forth already, this is the appropriate moment. Be sure to allow time in the morning schedule for negotiations, should they become necessary. The following should be done to end the day.

1. Ask for early acceptance, one week maximum. Mention that you will be seeing other candidates but would like to go ahead with this one; emphasize "we need to know soon."
2. The manager should present his business card and phone number, both at business and home, in the event that the candidate has further questions to ask.
3. Offer the candidate a confirming letter. If possible, have it typed and prepared to give the person before he leaves the site.
4. Mention physical examinations, if required.
5. Have host and hostess facilitate candidate's departure, picking spouse up at the hotel, getting to the airport, and waiting until the plane departs.

6. Write a warm follow-up letter. This letter could mention again the main points indicated earlier, that is, that the company likes the candidate, needs the candidate, and believes the candidate will succeed. Mention should also be made of the spouse and that the manager believes the spouse and family will fit into the community and find it enjoyable.

Results of This Approach

A large chemical organization made a careful study of this selling approach, because it had the problem of filling many vacancies in locations that were physically unattractive or remote. The company obtained an extremely high acceptance rate of 80 percent to 90 percent. It was pleased to discover, too, that it made very few mistakes in selection. An indirect benefit from this method of selling a candidate is that it can strengthen a feeling of esprit de corps in the organization because key people are involved in the hiring and integration of a new person.

Summary

This chapter deals with some factors to be considered in trying to sell the candidate, particularly when the location or the industry is not particularly attractive or in vogue. It stresses satisfying the hidden needs of candidates, as well as the obvious overt needs. A format was provided for a thirty-six hour visit. A strong recommendation was made to include the spouse of the candidate in this visit and to focus on how the person will fit in the organization and the community. This is accomplished by providing opportunity for the candidate to have close contact with persons of similar background, age, and life-style.

CHAPTER 11

Matching the Candidate to the Job

Once the interview is completed, time has come to compare the candidate's qualifications with the demands of the job. As you may recall, the information from the interview should be organized into a balance sheet of the major strengths and limitations (a compilation of the confirmed hypotheses). In addition, it is recommended that a paragraph or two be written about the appliant's capabilities on each of the four basic factors—intellect, knowledge-experience, personality, and motivation. An example of a format for organizing the interview findings is shown in Figure 11.

The data in the summary paragraphs and the balance sheet should describe how the applicant functions—how he or she thinks, solves problems, relates with others, is motivated, and applies knowledge and experience. This description must be compared to the behaviors required to succeed in the job in question. For example, in fast-paced jobs, a behavioral description about one aspect of the work might read: "must be able to think quickly on his feet, be decisive, and make good judgments on the spot." In this job, anyone who was evaluated from the interview as being a "cautious, deductive thinker" might not be successful (depending, of course, on the applicant's other strengths and limitations).

Thus, the entire job can be described in terms of necessary, critical behaviors that account for successful performance. The more the overlap of the interview findings with the behavioral specifications, the more suitable the candidate. Obviously, there will rarely be 100 percent congruence, so good judgment must take over from technique or methodology.

The lack of a carefully delineated description of successful job behaviors significantly reduces accuracy in predicting job success. No matter how well trained and perceptive the interviewers may be, conflicting opinions and wrong decisions are likely to result if decision makers have differing views as to what is required for successful job performance. For accurate identification of the candidate most likely to succeed, it is absolutely essential that the job be defined in behavior terms. This kind of description is known as behavioral specifications.

It is important to distinguish between behavioral specifications and other job data that could be used to understand the job (in order to make the candidate-job comparison). Two typical job information sources are job analyses and job descriptions. Both of these tools can be helpful in learning about the job, but they rarely provide the information needed to make a good selection decision. These sources do not describe the position in terms of necessary job behaviors. A review of both these sources and their use in the selection process follows.

Job Analysis

In large corporations, personnel experts often perform job analyses in which they describe the essential skills and knowledge required for certain positions. While these analyses can be helpful in screening applicants for tasks that require definite measurable skills such as for stenographers or machine operators, their value for analyzing management positions is doubtful. Knowledge and skill represent only a portion of the spectrum that determines effective performance in managerial or professional positions, and it is often difficult to analyze the exact skills and training needed. The talents exhibited by successful managers vary greatly from

FIGURE 11.   Format for organizing interview findings.

APPLICANT ASSESSMENT

NAME _____ EEO CODE _____ SEX _____

POSITION _____ DEPT. _____ JOB CODE _____

APPLICANT SOURCE _____ DATE _____

INTERVIEWED BY _____

STRENGTHS	WEAKNESSES

FIGURE 11. (*continued*)

INTELLECTUAL CAPACITY

KNOWLEDGE AND EXPERIENCE

MOTIVATION

PERSONALITY

OVERALL ASSESSMENT

For Initial
Position

Outstanding   Above Average   Average   Below Average

Growth
Potential

Outstanding   Above Average   Average   Below Average

ASSESSMENT SUMMARY (a brief, narrative evaluation of candidate)

RECOMMENDED ACTION (If rejected—reason for being rejected—be specific)

person to person, and the specific talents required for good management peformance are often as much a function of the industry and the nature of the company—its climate and its place in its own growth cycle—as they are indigenous to the job itself. Consider, too, the nature of the manager's position; that is, a manager usually has support staff or subordinates who compensate for his own deficiencies. For example, an executive with a perceived weakness in planning can be quite successful because a staff assistant who helps schedule and set priorities offsets this shortcoming. Thus a job analysis of all the skills and knowledge needed for a management or professional position is not likely to prove helpful in matching the man to the job.

Job Description

In addition to an analysis of skills and knowledge required for a certain position, the executive can also obtain a written job description. Such a description defines the tasks that the employee will have to perform. However, as with a job analysis, it does not provide the data needed to make the employment decision. First of all, job descriptions are usually prepared for salary administration purposes; that is, they assist salary administration experts in assigning a grade point value to each particular job, so that appropriate salary ranges can be established. These descriptions refect the tasks that the incumbent must carry out, but they rarely describe in meaningful terms the skills, talents, and aptitudes required. In essence, a job description only outlines the scope and functions of the job and defines the responsibility and authority of the incumbent.

A second reason job descriptions are not particularly useful in matching the applicant and the job is that they are static in nature. They may or may not reflect current conditions.

Finally, job descriptions do not describe the extra-job factors that affect the success of any manager. These include such elements as the personality dynamics of one's supervisor, the company pressures and climate, and the talents and personalities of subordinates.

Despite the limitations of job descriptions, it should not be concluded that a review of a written description is inappropriate. Review of a job description can help the executive to recall all the tasks to be performed. However, reliance on this tool as the only vehicle for understanding what is required would be inappropriate.

Behavioral Specifications

Behavioral specifications depict the job in terms of how the incumbent must function in order to perform successfully. It is not a question of what duties the individual must perform, but rather the manner in which they need to be carried out. Some behavioral specifications are written in terms of how the incumbent must not function and others, of course, in terms of the behaviors required. Figure 12 shows an example of a list of behavioral specifications drawn up for a district sales manager position.

In examining the behavioral specifications for the district sales manager, note that the framework for writing the specifications is on the basis of the four factors that account for job success. Notice, too, how the required behaviors can readily be compared with the conclusions from the interview, which are in the form of confirmed behavioral hypotheses. Figure 13 shows the sequence in the selection process.

Some general principles should be considered before we describe the data to be considered for developing the behavioral specifications.

Don't overqualify. Most managers tend to overestimate what is required to do a given job. Education is a good example. For many managerial jobs, it is categorically stated that the incumbent must be a college graduate. In reality, however, the course materials studied and completed for a college degree may be irrelevant for successful performance of the manaerial tasks. Of course, the attainment of a college degree may indicate something about the applicant's intellec-

FIGURE 12.   Example of behavioral specifications.

JOB TITLE: District Sales Manager

REPORTS TO: Regional Sales Manager

KEY RESPONSIBILITIES

Directs activities of eight sales supervisors.

Maintains direct contact and control over six key accounts.

Develops methods and programs to assist sales supervisors train
sales representatives.

Recruits and hires sales representatives to adequately staff the district.

Critical Behavioral Specifications

KNOWLEDGE AND EXPERIENCE FACTORS

Minimum of one-year experience in retail grocery trade.

Minimum of one-year experience in supervising salesmen—needs good
insight and trial-and-error experience in directing others.

Needs good knowledge of sales techniques and principles.

Must have valid driver's license.

INTELLECTUAL FACTORS

Needs to be able to solve problems at college graduate level—most
subordinates and buyers will be college graduates.

Must have good verbal skills—should be able to express self effectively
in face-to-face situations.

Needs to be decisive—must make many quick decisions in field.

MOTIVATIONAL FACTORS

Must like extensive people contact in everyday work.

Must find satisfaction in physical mobility—not a desk job.

Must have high achievement needs—should show evidence of being a
self-starter—will have very limited field supervision.

Must have good energy level—show evidence of being able to travel
and work long hours.

Should have ambition to advance up sales ladder—must be able to
advance at least to regional manager.

PERSONALITY FACTORS

Needs to be warm, affable, and outgoing—must make good initial
impression.

Must be able to cope with frustration—should be able to roll with
punches—will be subject to many frustrating sales situations.

FIGURE 13. *Block diagram of selection process.*

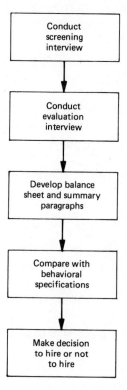

tual interests or abilities, but all the topics covered in a degree program do not have application in many jobs. The executive should think carefully before deciding how to define the body of knowledge considered necessary for the job.

A good way to check whether or not a specification is really essential is to see how many successful individuals currently employed (performing in the job in question) actually manifest the particular behavioral specification. Another similar check would be to ask, "How many of our best employees now doing this job would be hired if we used thse behavioral specifications as the criterion for the job offer?"

Don't overstress technical qualifications. The need for specific technical know-how diminishes as a function of organizational level. Moreover, rapidly changing technology results in quick knowledge obsolescence. The applicant is going to be either a technician or a manager—rarely can one be good at both. If effective management is desired, technology should be of relatively less importance.

Behavioral specifications should be present- and future-oriented. "They should be oriented, first, to the situation now existing in the company and in the outside managerial market. They should also be oriented toward the future, toward the corporation's long-range goals, toward the likelihood of change in managerial needs and attitudes. By all means, they should ignore the past—and failure to do so is a fault that most companies are addicted to. The fact that the company president was born in a log cabin is no justification for requiring all future presidents to be born in log cabins. We are exaggerating, of course, to emphasize the futility of hiring what has been successful in the past. Data from research should be evaluated only in terms of what they portend for the future." [1]

Writing Behavioral Specifications

As mentioned earlier in this chapter, behavioral specifications are written for each of the four basic factors that account for success at work. They require the description of needed knowledge and methods of functioning on the job. Most managers should not find these specifications difficult or time consuming to write. Many management groups have said to me, "We just can't agree among ourselves about what's really important in this job." These same individuals, however, after a little instruction about writing behavioral specifications, found to their surprise that agreement was not difficult. The secret, if there is one, is to limit the list of specifications to those that are absolutely essential. To keep the list realistic and meaningful, ask, "If the candidate were not able to do this (specification) or did not possess this quality, could he or she successfully perform in the job?" If the answer is yes, then that element should not be included

[1] Felix M. Lopez, *The Making of a Manager* (AMA, 1970), p. 169.

among the list of behavioral specifications. Usually no more than fifteen will be listed. All the other qualities or skills that one might like to list are no doubt good attributes to have, but they are not essential and will confound the decision-making process.

It is also helpful to keep in mind that the specifications should be specific in the sense that they describe knowledge of behaviors needed; they should not simply be a list of adjectives. For example, to write "mature" is not adequate. If maturity is an essential specification, then it should describe the behaviors needed such as, "must come across to others as professional—not appear kiddish, hucksterlike, or overly aggressive."

Following are some guidelines about how to write the specifications for each factor area. Also included are a few questions that may help in formulating the critical behaviors and know-how.

Knowledge and Experience Factor

The manager must avoid the temptation to describe knowledge and experience requirements in general terms, rather than focus on specific elements that are absolutely necessary. For example, a meaningful behavioral specification for a training director might read, "must have sufficient knowledge of current training techniques such as sensitivity training and confrontation methods to evaluate cost-effectiveness of programs offered by consultants." Two specific questions should be considered in describing knowledge and experience behavioral specifications.

First, "Is there any particular body of knowledge that the incumbent must have in order to carry out the functions of this job?" In answering this question, consideration must be given to whether or not the knowledge can be acquired on the job. The interviewer should also consider whether or not the know-how can be supplemented by subordinates or others in the company, such as staff experts. Often the potential to learn is more important than what has been learned.

The second question is, "What particular kinds of experiences would be necessary for effective performance in the job in question?" For many management assignments, the response has to be prior managerial experience at a specific level. Usually what is needed is the maturity that comes from exposure to problems similar to those that the manager will encounter in the new assignment. It often is not necessary that applicants have specific experience in the same industry or field of endeavor. There are many instances in which nontechnically trained individuals have successfully managed high-technology operations. In these assignments, many doubted that nonengineers could successfully manage the groups, and yet because of their excellent ability as managers, they were highly successful.

Motivation Factor

What will the incumbent be doing most of the time in the job? Planning? Directly supervising others? Solving complex technological problems? Whatever it is, specifications can be drawn about the activities the manager should *like to do* in order to be motivated in this assignment; that is, specifications can spell out what the incumbent's interests must be. For example, let us examine a research and development job in which the incumbent often spends much time alone monitoring a pilot plant operation. A motivation specification for this kind of job might read, "life history should show enjoyment in independent or solitary activities." Another specification could be, "incumbent should have a strong preference for working with concrete, tangible results as opposed to abstractions."

In general, the behavioral specifications should include two or three kinds of activities that a person would probably have to like doing in order to find the work tasks satisfying. Referral to the discussion of interests in Chapter 3 may prove helpful here.

In writing motivational specifications, thought also should be given to the goals and objectives that should be manifested in the applicant. Many positions tend to be dead-ends. Consequently, specifications must indicate the extent to which the applicant can have ambitions for further advancement. A specification for a position in which advancement cannot be rapid might read, "applicant needs to be willing to invest at least two years' development time in the

Wilmington plant before promotion to the director of manufacturing position."

Some questions to think about when determining the specifications for the motivation factor are, What should the applicant like to do if he or she is going to enjoy working in this job? Is there anything the applicant definitely should not dislike doing? Are any goals or aspirations essential? Does the job require any unusual energy demands (long hours or constant travel)? How critical is the drive level? Must the incumbent overcome many obstacles?

Personality Factor

Are any particular personality qualities essential for success in this assignment? This is often a difficult question to answer. The temptation is to list such obvious qualities as initiative, decisiveness, self-confidence, and so forth. Rarely, however, are these meaningful specifications except when these qualities are necessary in the extreme. Remember that whether a trait is helpful or not depends in large measure upon the other traits with which it is combined in the individual. Thus it is more helpful to look at specific issues relating to personality strengths and limitations when considering possible specifications.

How much pressure is inolved in this job? Does the incumbent need ability to roll with the punches? In analyzing possible sources of pre sure, the interviewer should examine the number and importance of deadlines, the extent to which pressing demands are made on the incumbent by others, and the number and nature of internal conflicts.

Does the person need to be reflective or action-oriented? Is the type of work best managed in a cautious, analytical way, or is it important to get things done immediately? If the former situation prevails, the behavior specifications might indicate that the applicant should manifest a behavior pattern that is characterized by reflectiveness, restraint, and caution. For an action-oriented job, the specification might read, "incumbent should be highly energetic and be able to make decisions under pressure."

Does the incumbent need to be socially dominant? Will there be many conflicts with others—subordinates, peers, or supervisors? Is a strong dominant personality needed to minimize being buffeted about by conflicts and pressures? Here are some additional questions to think about when determining the specifications for the personality factor: Are any essential personality qualities needed for success in this job? How must the incumbent handle stress or pressure? What kind of interpersonal behavior is required to perform the job—if any? Up the line? Peer level? Down the line? Outside the organization (customers and others)?

Intellectual Factor

How critical are communication skills for success in the job? For most management positions, the specification will probably read, "must express self well, both in writing and in face-to-face situations." The behavioral specification should note the kind of communication skills that need to be demonstrated. In many technological assignments, communication in writing, for example, is far more critical than ability in face-to-face encounters.

How complex is the task to be performed? The requirement for intellectual capacity depends in large measure on the number of variables the individual must consider in decision-making activities. The Peter Principle—that people rise to the level of their incompetence [2]—has validity for the very reason that many managers get in over their heads because of inability to cope with additional variables they encounter in new assignments. If the job being studied is narrowly circumscribed, high capacity for dealing with many variables may not be necessary.

Some questions that can be asked to help formulate specifications for the intellectual factor include, Are any specific intellectual aptitudes necessary (for example, math or mechanical)? How should the candidate go about problem solving (off the top, cautious, deductive)?

To assist the executive in preparing a list of behavioral specifications, a worksheet entitled "Developing Behavioral Specifications" is shown in Appendix C.

[2] Laurence J. Peter and Raymond Hill, *The Peter Principle* (New York: William Morrow & Company, 1969).

FIGURE 14.   Behavioral specifications for a sales trainee position.

Knowledge/Experience:

1. Ranks high (upper half) in sales knowledge test.
2. Has had demonstrated success in persuading others.

Motivation:

1. Shows good internal drive and push—evidence of at least one self-starting activity incident.
2. Shows evidence of high energy level and strong competitive nature.
3. Likes mobility—at least doesn't mind travel or moving about—not desk type.
4. Likes people contact.

Personality:

1. Must be socially outgoing (seen in interview and past activity).
2. Optimistic attitude—at least shows no evidence of discouraging easily.
3. Shows evidence of ability to sustain long-term relationships.
4. Evidence of persistence and perseverance.

Intellectual:

1. Must be able to communicate (written and verbal) at level acceptable to customers and company management.
2. Shows approach to problem solving in a broad scope, rather than narrow and detailed manner.
3. Innovative—shows flexibility in thinking and approaches to problems.

In Figures 14, 15, and 16 are three more examples of behavioral specifications developed by managers in their respective companies. These lists may suggest how behavioral specifications can be assembled.

FIGURE 15.   *Behavioral specifications for pharmaceuticals field representative.*

I. Knowledge/Experience

Two to four years of field sales experience.
Must have
- Closed sales.
- Worked variety of customers.
- Managed self in field.
- Handled finances.

or

Knowledge equivalent to that gained through two to four years' experience.
- Ability to talk effectively with veterinarians in animal health of pharmaceuticals industry.
- Ability to communicate effectively with college-level personnel—college degree or evidence of equivalent ability.

Valid driver's license.

Experience of successful management of personal finances.
- No evidence of significant financial mismanagement.

II. Intellectual factor

- Good ability with numbers—needs to be able to calculate price/dosages and percentages.
- Communicates easily, logically in face-to-face situations; does not seem at a loss for words or disorganized.
- Must be able to communicate sufficiently well to write effective letters to customers.
- Must not show evidence of inability to make decisions frequently or of poor judgment or planning.

III. Motivation factor

- Must like extensive contact with people.
- Must like to travel, at least not dislike it.

□ Must like being on his own and show some evidence of independent self-starting.

□ Desirable to show some evidence of liking to engage in competitive activities (cards, sports).

IV. Personality factor

□ Must not show evidence of inability to handle pressure.

□ Must come across to others as professional, not as a huckster or immature.

□ Must appear to care about others, show ability to empathize, and convince others of sincerity.

□ Must appear self-confident in interview.

An Important Consideration

One reason little attention has been given to examining what is required by the job is that so many different kinds of individuals can perform any given task—and perform it successfully. The variations with which most professionals or managerial tasks can be approached suggest that any definition of what is required to perform a job be undertaken in a cautious and conservative way. To be sure, matching abilities to the job requires some appreciation of what it may take to perform the job successfully. But the danger is great that the interviewer may come to believe that particular skills, traits, or aptitudes are essential, whereas, in reality, varying combinations of attributes will also result in successful job performance.

The interviewer should recognize that most evaluators tend to hire people who satisfy the overall needs of the company rather than to seek a variety of individuals who in combination fulfill company needs. For example, if executives were asked to delineate the ideal characteristics for a good manager in their firm, they might say:

□ "We want him to be creative but not too blue-sky."

□ "We want him to be practical and down to earth but not just a nuts-and-bolts man."

FIGURE 16.   *Behavioral specifications for bank management trainee.*

Intellectual

Demonstrate ability to learn technical and business information at college-graduate level, usually by completion of college degree.

Show evidence of solving problems in analytical, detailed manner and not gloss over things.

Show good insight about motivation and behavior of others.

Knowledge/Experience

Knowledge of business practices through actual business experience or business management courses.

Personality

Evidence of ability to wear well. Demonstrate ability to maintain long-term relationships with groups.

Must make a good initial impact on others—"come across" as poised and mature.

Show evidence of ability to adapt to rapidly changing situations (flexibility).

Demonstrate ability to be overtly enthusiastic.

Motivation

Evidence of persistence—or at least not be one who gives up easily.

Should show interest in (satisfaction in) being helpful to others—or at least not dislike it.

Express desire to advance to management level.

Evidence of self-starting ability. Will need to assume much initiative in branch locations.

- □ "We want him to be a good planner, but he also needs to be action-oriented."
- □ "He should be very bright but not so advanced that he cannot communicate and identify with those around him."

And so it goes. It is true that the company could not effectively use all creative thinkers, any more than it could be successful if it were composed entirely of action-oriented individuals. A successful company needs these skills but needs them in balanced proportions. As David A. Whitsett, a professor at the University of Northern Iowa, points out, the tendency is to seek the balance in each individual hired. Thus unusually creative persons are passed by because they are not practical enough or careful, conceptual planners are passed by because they do not get things done fast enough. Much thought should be given to meeting the company's needs through the diversity of its personnel rather than by trying to find this balance in one person. The company that consistently hires individuals with a balanced range of talents—none of which are extraordinarily developed—is likely to end with a static organization. It will often become a company composed of good mediocrity, but it will find itself losing out on the innovative thrusts and perceptive changes of direction that usually emanate from the not-too-well-rounded mavericks.

Thus it may not be so important that overall company requirements be mirrored in each specific job candidate. Job tasks can be shifted, incumbents can team with others to supplement deficiencies or augment strengths, and interplay among relatively narrow-gauged, highly talented personnel can also produce an effective coordinated whole.

Summary

This chapter introduces a new concept for defining jobs—behavioral specifications. These describe the essential knowledge and behavior patterns that must be evident for an incumbent to successfully perform a particular job. They help increase the accuracy of employment decisions because they are the ruler against which the interview findings are compared. Having a consistent frame of reference against which to measure applicants helps ensure more objective decision making.

Behavioral specifications are written on each of the four basic factors that account for job success. Mention was made of the need not to overqualify, overstress technical qualifications, or focus too much on past success patterns. In developing specifications, consideration must also be given to future direction of the organization.

CHAPTER 12

Sources of Candidates

Effective assessment techniques are most helpful when there is a pool of good talent from which the most qualified can be selected. This chapter provides a description of some of the usual, major sources of talent, as well as a few that are often overlooked. Some pointers are also provided for making optimal use of these sources. Campus recruiting is not discussed in this chapter. It will be explored in detail in Chapter 13.

Employment Agencies

Employment agencies are regulated by state laws (licensed) and really represent the job seeker. Because they need employment opportunities for their candidates in order to earn their fees, agencies aggressively contact potential employers to learn about present and future personnel needs. As an employer, you also may list job openings with agencies. In large cities, many agencies specialize in certain occupations such as sales, personnel, computer programming, bookkeeping, or nursing.

Agencies work on a contingency basis. That is, a fee or charge is not incurred until a candidate referred by the agency is actually hired. Agency fees vary greatly, from 1 percent per $1,000 of salary up to 25 percent of total compensation. The maximum fees are usually controlled by the state in which the agency operates. In some agencies, the employer pays no fee; the cost is met by the individual seeking employment. When many jobs need to be filled, or when an organization makes extensive or exclusive use of the agency, it is often possible to negotiate lower fees or make other arrangements to improve the cost-effectiveness of this recruiting source.

Most employment agencies operate on a percentage philosophy, that is, "if we send enough résumés to the client, eventually a match will be found and we'll place somebody." For company personnel departments and employers, this often means that you, not the employment agency, are doing the actual screening. For the fees being paid, you deserve more. The employment agency should refer only qualified applicants for you to interview. This will not occur, however, unless you demand it. In working with employment agencies, the word *demand* is well taken. Managers must be absolutely firm in pointing out to the agency personnel that they want to see only individuals who meet specified criteria and if nonqualified candidates are referred, use of their services will be terminated. The impact of this threat, of course, depends somewhat on the volume of business you do with the agency and the availability of other options in your community.

It is recommended that you develop behavioral specifications for each of the jobs to be filled and communicate these specifications to the agency, indicating which items are absolutely critical. The agency should be informed that unless the essential background and required job behaviors are clearly evident in the applicant, you do not want to see his or her résumé. You must be realistic and also be certain that your demands are in compliance with Equal Employment Opportunity regulations.

When working with agencies, it is also important to be aware that unless proper precautions are taken you could be obligated to pay a fee for candidates you or your organization may have solicited from other sources. The situation arises, for example, when someone sends you an unsolicited résumé, or perhaps one of your employees turns in a friend's completed application blank. The next day you receive from the employment agency a résumé describing the same person. If you hire that individual, the agency will claim the fee for "finding" the employee. It is important, therefore, to require the agency to give you the names of all candidates before their résumés are sent to you. At the same time, this list of names should be reviewed against all in-house applications or résumés currently in the company's possession.

Another step that can be taken to preclude that problem is to make one person or group within your company responsible for dealing with employment agencies. Let that person or group be the sole contact with the agencies with responsibility for flow of candidates and for fee negotiations.

Advantages of Using Agencies

Speed. Agencies can often provide many applicants rather quickly—something that is especially helpful if there is an urgent need to fill an opening.

Privacy. Use of an agency allows your company to go into the job market and keep the company name or job opening confidential (at least until the first candidate is interviewed).

Research. Study of candidates sent by agencies can often help determine the nature of the labor pool available to fill certain jobs as well as average salary costs, and the like.

Disadvantages of Agencies

Aggressive "sell." Employment agencies are often criticized because of unprofessional behavior on the part of some of their employees. Many have been known to try to sell employers candidates who do not meet the job requirements.

Not for higher management. Employment agencies are not suitable as sources of top management assignments. Usually, employment agencies work on jobs at the lower salary levels, although many now actively place individuals at middle management and professional levels, such as engineers, personnel managers, computer experts, and sales managers.

Executive Search Firms

Most reputable executive search firms perceive themselves as consultants to the clients they serve. Unlike the employment agencies, search firms are engaged by the employer, not the job seeker. Thus, they are hired to seek out and present to their clients candidates who meet desired specifications. Most search firms are organized to find candidates at professional, upper-middle, and top management levels. Difficult-to-find candidates, such as those with special technological skills, also make up a portion of the business for most search firms.

Executive search companies charge 25 to 30 percent of the recruited person's first year compensation; out-of-pocket travel and search costs can run between 10 and 25 percent of the search fee and are billed in addition to the basic fee. Unless you have been a long-term client, most executive search firms will not accept assignments for jobs paying less than $25,000 a year. However, some firms may take the assignment for relatively low-paying jobs for a negotiated fee that is not related to the incumbent's compensation level.

Working with a Recruiter

The first task, obviously, is to find a search firm that can do a professional job for you. This field is easy to enter, so it is filled with a large number of one- and two-man shops, some of which are highly competent, whereas others disappear almost as quickly as they appear. Unless you personally know the background or reputation of the very small, independent search group, the safer course of action is to consult the Directory of the Association of Executive Recruiting Consultants, Inc.[1]

The executive search business is in many ways dominated by a Big Six. These firms account for approximately 30 percent of all searches, and it is estimated that they account for more than 50 percent of the searches involving positions paying at least $100,000 a year. While each of these Big Six (Russell Reynolds Associates, Boyden Associates, Spencer Stuart & Associates, Heidrick & Struggles, Korn/Ferry, and Egon Zehnder International) claim to be unique, they all use basically the same process. First, they determine a descrip-

---

[1] Association of Executive Recruiting Consultants, Inc., 30 Rockefeller Plaza, New York, N.Y. 10020.

tion or profile of the executive the client desires. They locate and present several individuals who closely fit the profile, assist in negotiations, and then aid the company in persuading the candidate to take the offer.

Other sources are some of the major public accounting firms and management consultants. If your firm already employs one of these consulting organizations, it often can be effective in finding just the right candidate, since it may already be knowledgeable about your company and its operations.

In selecting a search firm it is advantageous to obtain the appraisals of business associates who have used various firms. Invite several search firms to make a presentation to you about their fees, approach, track record, experience in recruiting the type of job you are trying to fill, and who will actually be in charge of the search. This last point is important. For the presentation, the larger firms are likely to send a top-level officer, who in most cases will be impressive. However, the actual search work and liaison between you and the search organization may be with a junior staff member who does not attend the presentation meeting. In working with a search organization, the kind of relationship (openness and ease of communication) you establish with the specific recruiter handling the search is extremely important and should not be underestimated.

Once the firm has been selected, the most important single step you can take is to be clear in your own mind about what kind of candidate is desired. All recruiters will interview you about the job requirements, but it is the preparation for these discussions that matters. Carefully thought-out behavioral specifications can be most helpful. If these are prepared in writing for the recruiter, there can be no question about your expectations. Explain to the recruiter that as he or she presents the background of candidates, you will expect him or her to describe to you how the candidate does or does not fulfill the specifications. Such a procedure should help you decide whether or not you want to invest time to interview the candidate. Sometimes, when recruiters use their own format for presenting a candidate, a smooth presentation and highlighted strengths may make the candidate appear extremely attractive; yet, on critical analysis, the individual may not be able to do the job you want accomplished.

Be realistic. Sometimes, a company approaches recruiters with the attitude that because these people are professionals, and because it is paying them a lot of money, it will make them "shoot for the stars" and find the perfect candidate. While the goal is admirable, it usually is self-defeating. Of course, there is no perfect candidate. As in purchasing new sailboat, it is often a matter of finding the best compromise—trading one feature off for another. The essential question always must be, "Can the candidate do the job?" All kinds of people can succeed, depending on the unique blend of qualifications they bring, as long as they function as the behavioral specifications demand.

Be realistic about compensation. Most recruiters have an excellent feel for what it will take to recruit top personnel for the job you are trying to fill. Demanding top people but being unwilling to pay well will usually result in disappointing candidates and/or frustration.

It is also important to allow adequate time. Finding the best candidates is often a time-consuming process. Even if the recruiter personally knows of a good potential candidate, arranging a meeting, reviewing qualifications, and making comparisons with other candidates takes considerable time. The average time to complete a successful search is ninety days. If possible, don't wait to initiate the search until the need is desperate. A last-minute crisis approach often occurs after a company has exhausted all possibilities itself, has not developed the caliber of candidate wanted, and then calls in the professional recruiter.

Be frank and open with the recruiter. No consultant can do the best possible job for you unless he or she really understands the job, compensation, and environment in which the incumbent will be placed. For example, give the recruiter an opportunity to review key personnel to whom the incumbent will report (unless, of course, disclosure of the search will create internal organization problems). It is helpful for the recruiter to know, for example, whether the organizational climate is formal or informal, structured or relatively loose and free-flowing.

An interesting and creative approach to the use of search firms is to involve the subordinates of the potential incumbent to work closely with the executive recruiter in determining behavioral requirements. In this approach, the employees help select the individual who will be their boss.[2]

Advantages of Using Search Firms

Experience. Most professional recruiters have an extensive range of contacts that are personally known. Even more important, they know where the sought-after talent can be located. Each good search firm has developed its own system of identifying and tracking down desired candidates. In brief, these firms are in the business, searching every day, and know where and how to find people.

Confidentiality. Very often a company may wish to keep from its own employees or competitors that it is seeking to fill a key position. Frequently, too, it may wish to put out "feelers" to a particular person without a direct approach. In such cases, the recruiter can meet the candidate and discuss job opportunities with him or her without the company being identified.

Time. Recruiting top people is usually difficult. Most of them are engaged in jobs and careers that are already rewarding. Therefore, it is a matter not only of locating such people, but equally critical, of selling them on the job to be filled. Even getting potential candidates to listen about an opportunity over lunch is often difficult. The recruiter's greatest assistance is his ability to save the clients time by presenting for interview only qualified and interested candidates.

Disadvantages of Using Search Firms

There is an up-front risk in using search firms in terms of expenses. Most recruiters work on a one-third, one-third, and one-third basis. That is, one-third at the time you engage their service; one-third after one month; one remaining third at completion of the assignment. If, for some reason, the search firm cannot find your person, the investment is

[2] See "A Participative Executive Search" as listed in Selected Reading.

lost. Frequently, too, changes in the company often result in a decision not to fill the vacancy. In such instances the fee is also lost.

Advertising

We are referring here to classified ads in newspapers or block space advertisements in trade journals and/or newspapers. Advertising is difficult to evaluate because its effectiveness depends so much on the level of job and the impact of the advertisement. Media costs can run as little as $100 to more than $10,000, depending on the size of the ad, the frequency with which it is run, and the circulation of the publication. Considering the number of applicants advertisement can potentially raise, advertising is usually a cost-effective way to identify candidates.

Generally, advertising will provide a large number of résumés from candidates who will not meet your needs. For example, a consulting firm recently ran a block advertisement in the Sunday issue of *The Los Angeles Times*. Within a week, 248 replies were received. Of these, only five respondents were deemed sufficiently qualified to invite for an interview; however, one of those interviewed was hired.

Working with Advertisements

Most companies find that advertisements are most useful in producing good candidates when one or more of these conditions exist: (1) a large number of people need to be hired (for example, a new plant being put into operation); (2) the skill or job requirements are not stringent; that is, a wide range of individuals could perform the job; and (3) a specific, easily ascertainable skill or knowledge is required; that is, the advertisement performs much of the screening, such as advertising for an aircraft flight test engineer.

Most large organizations will find it productive to engage an advertising agency to develop and place their advertisements. Many of the larger advertising agencies have subsidiaries whose primary thrust is the development of effective recruiting ads. These specialized agencies can save much time and effort in determining the best media for the ad (newspaper, radio/TV, trade journal), developing the copy, and handling the placement, scheduling, and payment for the ads. If you employ an advertising agency to assist you, be certain that the final ad will always be submitted to you for approval. In this way any errors can be picked up, but more importantly, you can check it for discriminatory statements. Your legal responsibility does not end simply because an outside agency developed the copy.

Advantages of Advertising

Speed. Advertising can often yield a wide range of applicants rather quickly. If a large hiring is to take place with many jobs to fill, advertising may be the most efficient approach.

"Feel" of the market. Employers may often want to know what is out in the marketplace. The company may be considering, for example, expansion into a new product area, and wants to ascertain the availability of individuals possessing special technical skills. Thus, advertising about a job opening can serve as a form of market research.

Public relations. Frequent advertisements in which the company name is prominent can have a positive impact for future recruiting. Quality advertisements suggest that the company is growing and "on the move." The image of a company that is expanding and has growth opportunities often results in top people in competitive organizations coming forward without solicitation.

Disadvantages of Advertising

Attracts the disgruntled. One reason advertisements are frequently not productive is that the better candidates do not respond to them. Either they are happily employed elsewhere and therefore not likely to read the ad or, if they do observe it, they may be reluctant to expose themselves by responding to the advertisement (unless the ad reveals the company name and location). The business community abounds with tales of employees who revealed their discontent by responding to a blind ad (box number) only to discover the ad was placed by their own company—occasionally for their own job.

Screening problem. As suggested, the number of well-qualified applicants per hundred replies is likely to be low. Depending on resources available to review the mail or answer telephone calls, sifting through the responses could be burdensome, particularly if the company name is displayed. In such cases, good public relations would dictate that the applicant deserves some acknowledgement of receipt of his or her résumé. If only a box number is provided, then, of course, there is no need to reply.

Unsolicited Applications or Résumés

Without question, the most cost-effective way of recruiting personnel is through self-referrals or referrals by customers, employees, or friends of the company. Such applicants have two good qualifications: they want a job and they are interested in the company. Unfortunately, this potential pool of talent is often not capitalized upon. The persons who visit the firm or send in résumés in a steady stream often get lost in the shuffle, because at the time of their availability there is no appropriate vacancy. It is not uncommon for an executive who has been hired after a lengthy and costly search to indicate that he or she had an application with the company a few months earlier, but had never heard from anyone.

With easy access to computers in most organizations, there is little reason not to capitalize on this self-referral source of talent. It is relatively easy to keypunch essential data from résumés, which can then be matched against an in-house personnel requisition format. In this way, whenever a vacancy occurs, a pool of talent can quickly be searched for potential candidates.

Many companies find that an excellent source of candidates is referrals from current employees. Since these individuals already work in the company, they can often be effective recruiters in enticing others to join the firm. Also, since they go "on the line" when they make a recommendation to the company, they are likely to solicit only those individuals who will perform well or at the least not embarrass them by failure. In fact, a recent study of quit-rates found that employee referrals had significantly greater job tenure (stayed with the job for much longer periods) than referrals from employment agencies or newspaper advertisements.

To make good use of in-house company referrals, it is, of course, necessary to post job openings through company bulletin boards and house organs. Some companies offer employees recruiting awards or financial bonuses for individuals they recommend who are subsequently hired.

The advantage of this approach is that high-quality candidates may be found at low cost. The disadvantages are the possibility of ill will if an employee-recommended applicant is rejected, particularly if that person is a close friend of the employee, and the company's sacrifice of confidentiality if it posts the job opening.

Job Posting

Many organizations routinely post job descriptions and job requirements for employment opportunities within the company. Even if an organization does not routinely follow that practice, posting should be considered when trying to fill certain personnel needs.

Most companies find it impractical to list jobs at upper management levels because they want the latitude to bring in outside talent when necessary. Also, there is often a reluctance to publicize management openings, especially if significant organizational changes are planned. The cutoff point for using job posting in many organizations is at the level of lower-middle management. The exact level is usually defined in terms of salary grade.

The success of job posting in any organization depends largely on the personnel department's ability to constructively manage the volume of candidates the posting system may generate. The problem becomes acute because everyone who responds to the job opening should be talked with. Even those applicants who are obviously unqualified will need an explanation as to why they were not selected. If personnel is not staffed to conduct these turn-down interviews, there is high probability of engendering hostile feelings toward the posting system and/or the company. For an effective job posting program, it is essential at the outset to establish efficient procedures for evaluating employees who apply as well as constructively informing those not selected.

Organizations considering implementation of job posting need to make it clear that all jobs beneath a certain defined level must be posted when a vacancy occurs. This principle of all jobs being posted is critical to the success and integrity of any such effort and must be clearly understood at all levels in the organization. Failure to do so results in collapse of the system, because employees will pay little attention to it. When posted vacancies are filled by the most qualified individuals, regardless of what segment of the company they work in, employees feel good about job posting because it means that advancement possibilities are multiplied many times beyond those in their own work areas. However, when the policy is not firmly and consistently followed, employees believe that most jobs have already been filled by favored insiders.

Circumventing the posting program is often abetted by managers who wish to promote their own staff to vacancies in their respective departments. Managers are sometimes reluctant to open the door to unknowns from other areas of the company. This is the primary reason that clear and firm policies about posting are important and that it is essential to have a strong personnel department to implement the system.

Advantages of Job Posting

Builds morale. Managed properly, a job posting system clearly supports organization efforts to promote from within. It also offers promotional opportunities to the best employees (and helps retain them), even for those working in segments of the company in which there is little turnover or growth.

Uncovers talent. Because job posting requires that all who apply need to be at least considered, the system often uncovers some who are well qualified but might have been overlooked. It facilitates employees' career path changes.

Disadvantages of Job Posting

Demotivates. Unless employees who apply but are not selected are made fully aware of how they were lacking in comparison to the chosen candidate, the company will have one happy and five or six disgruntled employees.

Job posting requires a well-staffed personnel department to effectively administer the system.

Usually, the system is not appropriate for finding talent for upper-level management positions.

Summary

This chapter describes five sources of job candidates: employment agencies, executive search firms, advertising, self-referrals, and job posting. College recruiting will be discussed in depth in Chapter 13.

The method that a manager uses to find candidates depends upon the nature of the job to be filled (salary grade level and special requirements of the job) and the number of candidates needed. Often a combination of several recruitment sources is appropriate.

The most cost-effective method of finding candidates is self-referrals or referrals from current employees.

CHAPTER 13

College Recruiting—
A Game Plan

This chapter provides a detailed outline and guide for establishing and conducting an effective college recruiting effort. It is based on my personal experiences and those of countless client organizations. Despite the costs, college recruiting represents a major surce of talent for many organizations, especially those that are expanding or need a constant source of new professional or managerial talent.

Successful college recruiting depends upon careful preparation before the campus interview and management of the follow-up. This means that responsibility and authority must be clearly defined to achieve maximum results from the recruiting effort. A step-by-step game plan, including timing and accountability, follows.

Recruiting Manager's Responsibility

Whenever the company will be recruiting at more than a few campuses, it is essential that someone be responsible for the planning, organization, and coordination of the recruiting effort. At least ten crucial steps need to be managed. This responsibility should be assigned to a recruiting manager, who must be at a level in the organization that allows for control of a substantial budget and permits identification and selection of other company persons to be involved in the recruiting effort.

In the broadest sense, the recruiting manager is responsible for the following:

- Development of strong working relationships with campuses at which the company recruits.
- Determination of personnel needs for recent college graduates or graduate-level students and the best ways to obtain them.
- Development of an organization to carry out the recruiting function. This structure most often will include a steering committee and a group of executives, referred to as visit coordinators, responsible for specific recruiting activities at each school.

The Steering Committee

The steering committee should be composed of management representatives from the major operating units of the organization. Their primary responsibility is to determine the number and type of individuals, companywide, that need to be obtained from college sources. In addition, they often determine salary ranges to be offered, concern themselves with fulfilling Equal Employment Opportunity objectives, select the target schools for recruiting, and evaluate accomplishments of the recruiting effort. In some organizations the steering committee also organizes the structure of the initial jobs in which the recruits will be placed, as well as the design of development activities for the new college hires.

Visit Coordinators

Visit coordinators are responsible for the college relations and recruiting effort at a specific school. For the recruiting aspect of their job, they report directly to a member of the steering committee or the recruiting manager. Visit coordinators should be selected on the basis of their ability to cultivate faculty and students; often they are graduates of the school in question. These coordinators should be willing to devote at least two or three years to cultivating the school and its related organizations. Success in recruiting is not likely from a series of one-shot efforts. It requires a consistent, continuous effort that leads to a personal relationship between college placement officials, faculty, and the company's representatives.

Prerecruiting Preparations

Some factors to be considered in making the initial list of target schools are as follows:

1. Relevancy of the course curricula to company needs. For example, not all engineering schools are equally capable of developing good chemical engineers; some specialize more in electrical or mechanical engineering. Of pertinent concern is the number of graduates turned out each year in the company's area of interest.

2. Closeness of the college to the hiring location(s). The majority of college students attend schools within a 500-mile radius of their homes. The same reason that the student selected the college—preference for that geographic area and proximity to family or friends—may also be instrumental in the choice of employment location.

3. Extent to which faculty and others on campus think well of the company. What are the attitudes about your organization on campus? Faculty and administrators are affected by news events, sociological trends, and the like. For example, if one of the company's plants has recently been cited for an environmental violation such as water pollution, the faculty and students in that locality may have spoken out in negative terms about your organization. Recruiting visits to that campus might be an excellent beginning to change a negative image, but attitudes on campus sometimes determine which campuses to visit.

Obviously, once an organization has had recruiting experience at a particular school, the productivity of those recruiting efforts should be a major factor in the decision to continue or not continue recruiting on that campus.

Following are recommended time frames for prerecruitment planning elements.

Selection of schools. Unless the manpower needs dictate an extremely wide coverage of campuses, companies should carefully evaluate schools to be visited and target only those that are likely to be highly productive. This evaluation needs to be ongoing and revised from year to year, predicated on organization needs and experiences with the school.

Scheduling campus interview dates. Scheduling should be completed approximately twelve months before the actual visit. Many companies schedule the following year's visit dates while on campus for the current year's recruiting. Organizations seeking the most desired recruiting dates, late fall or January-February, may be relegated to late spring on the more popular campuses, unless dates are confirmed well in advance.

Forecasting requirements. Approximately six months before the visits begin and recruiting plans are established, manpower needs should be determined. In smaller organizations, often this is not much of a problem, but in large companies, the task is complex, involving correlation of needs with budget constraints and long-range corporate plans. Care should be taken, too, that personnel needs are not automatically allocated to college recruiting when in-house personnel might well meet some of the requirements (for instance, current employees who are completing evening undergraduate or graduate degree programs).

Development of recruiting materials. Three months before the first scheduled visit is about when the drafts of recruiting materials should be ready. These include brochures describing the company and its operations, interview report formats for campus interviewers, format of job offer and rejection letters, and an information packet for recruiters. This packet should contain organization charts, showing traditional lines of advancement in major areas of the company's operations; data about starting salaries and reasonable expectations for new employees after six months or a year of employment; and an outline of the specifics of the various benefits the company offers, vacation policies, and the like.

Development of plans for each campus. Two to four months in advance of the fall or spring recruiting dates, prerecruiting efforts should be planned and initiated. One aspect of this plan includes the determination of who will visit each campus. A number of different strategies have been found effective. Consider sending to the campus an employee who is a recent graduate of that college. Such a person might have much credibility with the students and can relate in a meaningful way his or her satisfaction with the company and its opportunities. Such a person may also know faculty members and can establish or reinforce a positive image of the company on campus. A risk is that relatively new employees may not be sufficiently knowledgeable of other operations in the company besides their own, but this shortcoming can be rather easily corrected.

Another approach that has been quite effective on some campuses to send as a recruiter someone who is competent and experienced, or who has progressed rapidly in the organization. This approach seems quite effective when recruiting candidates for high-technology areas. Such an interviewer is able to readily answer technical questions that may arise. Moreover, such a person may be a successful salesman for the company through an ability to excite or challenge the student by describing the technological problems in which the student may become involved by joining the company.

Another effective way to recruit is to send a team of two or more persons. In this way, it is possible to combine the advantages of a young recent graduate with the knowledge and experience of a longer-term employee. Another excellent combination is a line manager along with an experienced or professional interviewer, such as someone from the company's personnel department. This approach is discussed in more detail in Chapter 14.

Many organizations send professional interviewers to conduct the campus interview. These individuals are usually more effective than amateurs in screening candidates and, possibly because of their interview experience and human relations skills, are able to sell the company quite well. If many campuses are to be visited, however, this approach is not always practical.

If adequate manpower is available, a team of three or more can be effective on campus. It is not recommended that three or more be present for the actual interview, but activities of the larger team, both before and after the interview schedule, have been productive for many companies. Some of these activities are described in the following paragraphs.

A key element in developing a recruiting plan for each campus is the broader issue of overall relationship with the college. The single most important factor in successful college recruiting is the emphasis and care devoted to developing a year-round college relations program. It must be recognized that attitudes toward the recruiting organization make or break the recruiting for that company on the campus. One negative comment about an organization from a respected professor can easily result in none of the better students signing up. Positive attitudes, on the other hand, can do wonders in improving the number of top applicants that sign up for interviews. Following are some approaches that companies have used on an ongoing basis to stimulate positive interest in the company:

□ Advertising throughout the year in the college newspaper.
□ Visits to faculty members during the year, telling about new industry developments and sharing new technological publications and copies of books by company staff members or alumni.
□ Company offers of financial assistance to needy students.
□ Contributions to endowment funds.
□ Offering faculty members employment during the summer months.
□ Inviting faculty members to new plants or research centers for a firsthand look.
□ Making obsolete technical equipment or office equipment available to the university.

For a college relations program to be effective, the kinds of activities listed here cannot be sporadic; plans should be drawn so that these efforts are reasonably continuous and ongoing. This means that someone must be held responsible for the relations program on selected campuses. It is not surprising that companies which seem to get the cream of the crop usually have established excellent relationships with the faculty. Such firms typically designate someone to serve as college coordinator, and this individual initiates, coordinates, and directs all company contacts with the college.

Another aspect of the recruiting plan for each campus is the effort made to ensure that the most capable candidates sign up for the recruiting interviews. Such steps are geared to educate the students and faculty about the company and to create interest in the opportunities the organization offers. Several weeks before the scheduled recruiting visit, a company may sponsor an open house, during which representatives give a presentation about the organization and industry and conduct an open question-and-answer period. The open house may feature coffee and doughnuts or an elaborate cocktail party. Some attraction is usually needed to induce the students to turn out in large numbers. Such a social meeting provides an opportunity to promote the company in ways that are impractical during the regular interview procedures. Movies or slides can be shown, and faculty members should also be invited.

Another prerecruiting effort is to send letters or make phone calls to promising members of the graduating class, inviting them to sign up for an interview. Similarly, letters may be directed to faculty members, telling them of the visit, along with any specific or unusual opportunities the company may be offering. An example of such a letter (for students) is shown in Figure 17.

Training recruiters. An essential ingredient of any successful college recruiting effort has to be the skill of the interviewers, not only to assess, the best prospects but also to interest them in further contacts with the company through second interviews or meetings. It is folly to send to the campus managers who are not adequately prepared. Most organizations devote a full day to two days to this training, which should be scheduled a few weeks before the visits are to commence. Here are some topics that should be covered:

- Overall scope of the recruiting effort—manpower needs for the organization.
- Procedures for reporting interview appraisals, invitations for second interviews, and offering letters.
- Equal Employment Opportunity policies and company's compliance instructions.
- Techniques for conduct of the interview, along with ample opportunity to practice in class the techniques being taught.

FIGURE 17.   *Sample letter inviting candidates to sign-on schedules.*

Dear

We had an opportunity to review a résumé of your background and interests. Congratulations on your fine record.

Your interests seem to match with the opportunities here at
_____(company)_____. This year, as in the past, we are looking for a number of outstanding individuals to join our company. We believe you might have those excellent characteristics we seek. A copy of our literature is enclosed that describes our company and career opportunities.

We would like to invite you to our interview session scheduled for _____ at the _____
Placement Office. Your Placement Office will be able to supply you additional details regarding our visit.

I look forward to seeing you at that time and extend wishes for a successful final semester.

Cordially yours,

- Corporate promotional material that has already been distributed to campuses as well as that available for use during the visit.
- Data about progress and career path of typical young graduates hired during the past two or three years. Unless the recruiter is interviewing for only one or two job categories, it is helpful to have these profiles for a wide range of job entry points in the company.
- A list of typical questions asked by students along with suggested interviewer responses.
- Key facts about the company.
- A "walk through" of the annual report or other company literature, indicating significant highlights and/or areas that are likely to be questioned.
- Salary schedules—when and how deviations can be made from agreed-upon offered rates.
- Review of all company benefits particularly those of interest to young employees, such as tuition refund, compensation incentives, and so on.

During the training of campus interviewers, it is helpful to give them an opportunity to try out their interview procedures, by role playing or practice classroom interviews. Use of video tapes or, at the least, audio cassette tapes for feedback on the interview can be most helpful. Interviewers need to learn how to appropriately structure the twenty-five or so minutes of time available to them for the on-campus interview. Waiting until the interviewers arrive on campus is no time to start this practice. An outline for a recruiter workshop is shown in Appendix D.

Final review of personnel requirements. Manpower needs developed in the spring or early June have a way of changing when September comes. Therefore, at the outset of the recruiting cycle in September, the requirements for college-recruited personnel should be reviewed and the original recruiting objectives adjusted accordingly.

Conduct of campus interviews. Most of the interviews will be scheduled in October and November, and again in January and February. With many colleges now revising their academic calendar to finish the first semester by Christmas, December is replacing January as an important recruiting month.

The recruiting manager should be certain that dates are firm and that those persons scheduled to make the campus visit will be there at the time assigned to them. It is bad public relations for the company representatives not to show up for a scheduled interview day, unless ample notice has been given to the college placement office. For this reason, most organizations involved in college recruiting have a reserve of trained backup interviewers who can be called upon at the last minute to make the visit. Techniques for conducting the campus interview are described in Chapter 14.

Secondary interviews (company locations). The secondary interview is the one in which the hire, not-hire decision is made, and the evaluation model is employed at this time.

Within two weeks of the campus interview, a letter should be sent to all students interviewed, indicating an invitation for the secondary interview or a turndown. Sample letters for this step in the recruiting process are shown in Figure 18. The period between the campus interview and the secondary interview is critical in the process of recruiting. In fact, most recruiting efforts rise or fall on how the company manages the period of time before and after the secondary interview. It is critical, therefore, that all visits to any location clearly be the responsibility of a visit coordinator. This person should be accountable for the schedule of visits, all communications with the students, and the management of the applicant's time while at the company location.

If there is to be significant delay (four weeks or more) between the time of the invitation and the visit for the secondary interview, effort should be made to maintain contact with desired students. This communication can be achieved by follow-up letters, phone calls, or additional printed materials or literature about the company, such as a just issued annual report.

Once the student confirms an intention to visit for the secondary interview, the visit coordinator should send a letter to the student, indicating information about hotel ac-

FIGURE 18.   *Sample invitation and rejection letters (after campus interview).*

Dear

We are pleased to invite you to come to ___(company)___
_____ in _____(place)_____ , on _____(date)_____.
This will provide us an opportunity to get to know each other better and to explore our mutual interests about a career for you at _____.

Please contact _____(visit coordinator)_____ collect at
___(phone number)___ to confirm the above date. _(He/She)_
will provide additional details concerning travel and hotel arrangements at that time. Your visit will be at our expense.

I very much enjoyed meeting with you on my recent campus visit and am looking forward to seeing you again.

Sincerely yours,

Dear

Thank you for your interest in _____.
We truly appreciate the time you gave in discussing career opportunities with us.

It has been a difficult task to select the relatively few candidates from the large number of outstanding people interviewed. We have carefully reviewed your qualifications in order to explore a possible match between your talents and our needs. Unfortunately, we do not feel there is anything appropriate at this time.

We certainly enjoyed meeting and talking with you and wish you much success in your employment efforts.

Sincerely yours,

---

commodations, hotel bills, transportation information, company contact person on day of interview, and time needed for the interview. A sample letter for this information is shown in Figure 19.

It is usually effective to assign a sponsor or contact person who is designated as the applicant's companion for the day of secondary interviews. In most organizations, the sponsors are individuals selected for their ability to relate well with recent graduates. Often, sponsors are graduates who were

FIGURE 19.   *Sample letter confirming secondary interview (after secondary visit confirmed).*

Dear

We look forward to talking with you about career opportunities at _____
on _____(date)_____, in _____(location)_____.

Overnight reservations have been made for _____
evening, _____(date)_____, at _____(location)_____.
Transportation to the hotel can be arranged by _____.

_____ will meet you in the hotel lobby at 8 A.M. for breakfast and will bring you to headquarters to begin your day. During the course of your visit, we will make full reimbursement to you for all expenses associated with the trip.

We would appreciate it if you would complete the enclosed application and bring it with you at the time of your visit. If you have any further questions prior to your trip, please do not hesitate to call me collect at ____(telephone number)____.
Thank you again for the interest shown in _____;
I look forward to seeing you soon.

                              Sincerely yours,

hired through the company's recruiting process in the prior year or two. The role of the sponsor is to establish an informal, personal relationship with the candidates and to share with them enthusiasm for his or her job and the company. Sponsors frequently are called upon to meet candidates for breakfast at the hotel, drive candidates to the company facility, introduce candidates to visit coordinator or other company personnel, take candidates to lunch, take candidates on brief tour of facilities, and return candidates to homeward transportation.

The secondary interviews should be scheduled so as to have the fewest possible number of interviews. No data are available to demonstrate that a large number of interviewers produce more accurate predictions than fewer interviewers. When a candidate is being evaluated for several different departments or operations, three of four interviews of approximately forty-five minutes in length should be scheduled. More than four interviews, in most cases, should be unnecessary. As an alternative to the "beauty parade" approach, multiple interviews are recommended. Specific details on this subject are provided in Chapter 14.

Management of the secondary interviews requires much attention and advance planning by the visit coordinator. It is important that the interviews be handled in such a way that the candidate leaves with a positive impression of the company, whether or not an offer is given. Most college placement officials ask students to provide feedback concerning their visit, and a favorable student report can contribute substantially to the company's image on campus.

Visit coordinators should take steps to ensure that interviewers will

Be on time for scheduled interviews.

Be familiar with candidate's school, name of sponsor, and schedule for the day.

Cut off telephone calls and other interruptions.

Spend at least forty-five minutes in an interview, most of which should be evaluative.

Project a positive and enthusiastic picture about his/her career with the company.

To accomplish the foregoing usually means that the visit coordinator must provide training for interviewers concerning these expectations. In addition, they should learn how to conduct the evaluation model described in Chapter 9.

The individual scheduled for the last interview should escort the candidate back to the visit coordinator. At that time, the coordinator should settle expenses, explain the next steps, and inquire about any final questions the applicant may have. When all questions and administrative matters are settled, the sponsor usually takes the applicant to a transportation facility.

Making the offer. The offering decision should be made as quickly as possible once the interviews have been completed. Thus, offering letters are mailed throughout most of the recruiting period—January to April. A quick reaction from the company is a tangible way of showing interest and commitment to the applicant. A strong positive impact can be made, for example, if candidates leave the secondary interview with an offer in their pocket.

Usually, there is little advantage in delaying notification of turndowns unless it is known that several applicants from a given school will be visiting in close time proximity. Then, it may be advantageous to wait until all have had their secondary interviews before the offer or turndown letters are sent. A typical turndown letter is shown in Figure 20.

The offering letter. Obviously, each organization must tailor its letter to match its own style and to include the specific information it wishes to convey. However, most offering letters should include the following:

A strong, positive opening that indicates the organization was impressed by the candidate. It is particularly helpful if the letter can be tailored to mention a specific trait, skill, or quality of the candidate that impressed the interviewers.

Position and title of initial assignment.

Salary and benefits (and/or benefits brochure).

Contingencies: taking a routine physical examination prior to the starting date (if applicable).

Information regarding moving and relocation.

FIGURE 20.   Sample turndown letter (after secondary inter-view).

Dear

We enjoyed having you visit _____(name of facility)_____
and discuss career opportunities with some of our managers.

It has been a difficult task to select the relatively few candidates from the large number of outstanding people invited
to our facilities for second interviews. Your qualifications
were reviewed against our current needs and, unfortunately, we have decided to make offers to other individuals
whose background and interests more closely match these
needs.

We sincerely appreciate your interest in _____
_____ and wish you much suc-
cess in your career.

                                    Sincerely yours,

An indication of who will next contact the candidate.
An indication of when the company would like to have
    the candidate's decision.
A closing statement to solidify the organization's strong
    interest in the applicant.
A sample offering letter is shown in Figure 21.

Once the offer is made, continued contact is critical until
the time of acceptance or rejection. The contact is especially
essential with the better candidates who may receive many
attractive offers. Organizations have found that a show of
personal interest, concern, and genuine desire for the candidate to become an employee is often the determining factor
in an applicant saying yes. Sometimes, a turndown could
have been avoided if the hiring organization were aware of a
dilemma or problem facing the applicant. For example, the

FIGURE 21.   Sample offering letter.

Dear

This will confirm our conversation yesterday. We are pleased to offer you a position as ____(job title)____ in the _____at a starting salary of $_____ per year. In addition to your base salary, you will become immediately eligible for _____ and a variety of other group insurance and benefit programs which rank among the finest in industry. I've enclosed some descriptive material on these programs.

The company will reimburse you for the cost of moving your household furnishings to your new location. Reimbursement will also be made for your cost of transportation and meal and lodging expenses incurred en route. In addition, as a new employee, you are allowed up to 30 days' meal and lodging expenses at the new location while arranging for permanent quarters.

We understand that this is an important and difficult decision for you on the basis of your limited exposure to _____. I can only reemphasize the exceptional growth opportunities and exposure this position offers to you.

If there are any questions which you feel are unanswered, or if any arise, please feel free to call me collect. Further, if you believe another visit would be helpful in your arriving at a decision, please let me know and we will make arrangements.

I look forward to your accepting our offer.

                                        Sincerely yours,

candidate may have thought well of an organization's offer, but was not pleased by the location of the initial job. For many companies, switching initial job location may present no difficulty and would be worth doing in order to recruit the candidate. The recruiting manager must see that close contact is kept with the student and the placement office at the student's school.

Some important steps that should be taken, once the offer has been made, are as follows:

> Contact the student shortly after the offer has been made to offer congratulations, answer questions, and inquire if any additional information or help is needed.
> Contact the college placement office about the offer.
> Use mailings to maintain ongoing contact. Newsletters, house organs, speech reprints, telephone calls, and letters from the department head where the applicant is likely to be assigned are all appropriate.
> Encourage students to call collect for any reasons concerning their decisions.
> Offer to arrange another visit, if it appears necessary.
> Determine approximately when the student will be making the final employment decision.

Approximately one week before it is expected that the candidate will make the yes or no decision, the student should be contacted to determine if anything can be done to aid in reaching a positive decision. At this time, it is usually not appropriate, especially from the public relations standpoint, to engage in high-pressure tactics. Expressions of a personal desire to see the student join the organization and of concern for any questions or issues are most effective. One can also stress any truly unique aspects of an organization or job offer that the applicant is not likely to have received from competing companies.

Once an offer has been accepted, the recruiting manager should arrange for a congratulatory letter to be sent by the president or other high company official. In some organizations, this same executive indicates an interest in meeting the applicant once he or she is "on board." This letter also can reaffirm the starting employment date and location to which the candidate should report on the first day. A sample of such a letter is shown in Figure 22.

Follow-through after acceptance is also important. Students change their minds from time to time, so contact through suggestions made earlier in this section should be continued.

Postrecruiting. Once the recruiting season is over, the recruiting manager should assume responsibility for a number of significant steps. He should make an analysis of results (number of students recruited) for each of the schools visited. These figures, compared to costs of recruiting at each respective school, should help determine the efficiency of recruiting at that institution. Such an analysis can also help pinpoint weak elements in the recruiting effort, inadequately trained or incompetent interviewers, paucity of students for the requirements sought (perhaps the school is not the right one for the kind of candidates needed), poor follow-through, and negative attitudes toward the company by certain faculty members.

Within three months of employment, some follow-through on placement of new recruits and their satisfaction

FIGURE 22.   Sample welcome letter (after offer is accepted).

Dear

_____ informed me that you have accepted our offer and plan to join us this _____.
I am very pleased with your decision and hope _____ fulfills your career expectations.

I look forward to working with you, and if either _____
_____(recruiting manager)_____or I can do anything for you in the meantime, please let us know.

Sincerely yours,

with the company is recommended. In employment interviews, students often express career or location preferences, which the company tries to match, at least in the initial assignment. However, interests or life status (a marriage, for example) may change between the time of acceptance and employment. Also, the realities of the job or location may prove to be different from what the candidate expected. Given the high percentage of turnover among young college graduates and M.B.A.'s during the first two years of employment, early identification of problems among new recruits before they become entrenched in a significant, permanent job assignment could substantially reduce turnover.

Timetable for Key Steps in an Effective
Recruiting Process

Activity	Date	Responsibility
Source evaluation	Continuing	Recruiting manager
Schedule recruitment dates	Approximately 12 months in advance	Recruiting manager Steering committee
Identify needs for following year	July	Recruiting manager Steering committee
Review/develop recruitment materials	August	Recruiting manager
Develop college relations activity plan	September	Visit coordinators
Implement college relations activities	Ongoing	Recruiting manager Visit coordinators
Conduct college recruiting workshop	October/November	Recruiting manager
Conduct campus interviews	January/February	Recruiting manager Visit coordinators
Conduct second interviews	March/April	Recruiting manager; branch and home office management
Make offers	April/May	Recruiting manager
Evaluate program	August	Recruiting manager

Adjustments in career path and/or location are often relatively easy to accomplish during the first few months of employment, but not later on.

A timetable for key steps in managing an effective recruiting program is summarized in the table on page 198.

Advantages of College Recruiting

It is difficult to see many direct advantages to college recruiting. Many large corporations wish it would just go away but are forced into recruiting to get their share of bright young talent. It would appear, however, that recruiting is here to stay. Here are some advantages:

Corporate image. There are public relations benefits from the company being known by graduating students. Even if they are not recruited as young graduates, their positive attitudes toward the organization may predispose them to seek employment in the future or to accept an employment offer at a later time. Of course, these advantages could easily vanish if the college recruiter or the recruiting process is ineffective and leaves a bad impression with candidates.

"Big net" value. Campus recruiting may be the only viable way of hiring a pool of young college graduates. Many organizations have effective management development and training programs that prepare young employees for key responsibilities, and the college graduate represents the right mix of intelligence, age, and educational background for the company's development effort. A good example is seen in public accounting firms, especially the Big Eight. For these firms, a college education provides the foundation; firms teach the technical skills needed for educated recruits to perform as certified public accountants.

Disadvantages of College Recruiting

Cost. Cost per employee obtained is high. It is not difficult to see how the costs of campus recruiting become so high. In a recent informal survey among several major corporations, it was found that approximately twenty-five applicants were interviewed for each person actually hired. These interviews included the campus interview as well as the second interviews in the home office or plant location. When you consider management time in preparing schedules, training interviewers, visiting campuses, second interviews, travel costs, and administrative expenses, it is not difficult to see how the cost of recruiting can easily total several thousand dollars per hire.

High salaries for inexperienced talent. Because of the competitive aspects of campus recruiting, starting salaries are quite unrealistic, relative to the contribution these individuals can make, given their limited experience. So, in effect, hiring young graduates at competitive starting salaries is essentially an investment in the future. As it turns out for many organizations, it is an uneconomic investment, because the turnover of these young hires after two or three years is quite high. In a study recently conducted by the College Placement Council, one college recruit of every three hired left within three years. Of course, the turnover varies greatly from one organization to another. Each organization should take a critical look at what happens to their campus recruits after a two-year period—at the time when most of them are finally becoming productive enough to warrant their earnings. This situation is particularly aggravated in the case of M.B.A.'s; their leave rate before three years is even higher, with many clients reporting a 40 percent loss. While hiring good M.B.A.'s represents a challenge, it's an even greater challenge to keep them.

Summary

This chapter provides a comprehensive, step-by-step procedure for carrying out an effective recruiting effort on college campuses. One of the essential points covered is the importance of designating people who are responsible for coordinating the effort, for establishing good relationships with the colleges where the recruiting is to take place, and for providing adequate development and training of the recruiters who will do the interviewing.

A key element in the recruiting process is the management of the procedures to be used when the recruited candidate arrives for the secondary interviews at the home office, regional office, or plant.

The importance of showing personal concern and interest for the applicant is stressed. It is recommended that care be taken as to the nature of the evaluation forms used and that the paper process be kept minimal.

CHAPTER 14

College Recruiting— The Interviews

When hiring college seniors, the manager is likely to be engaged in two types of interviews—the one conducted on the college campus in order to recruit the applicant and interest him or her in the company and the second, the home office interview, in which the recruited student visits a company location. In the latter case, the primary purpose of the interview is to make a final hire, not-hire decision and to sell the student on coming to work for the company. Because each of these interviews presents special problems, both from the evaluation and procedural standpoint, they will be discussed separately.

There are significant differences between the campus interview and the kind of evaluation interview that has been described in this book. These differences center around the need to sell the company, the amount of time available, and the pressures placed on the interviewer. Because the campus interview places extra demands on the interviewer, a specially tailored interview approach must be used. However, before describing the guide or model for the campus interview, it may be worthwhile to examine these differences in greater detail.

The Need to Sell

Most interviews are conducted to help the executive make a hire, not-hire decision. This is not true of the campus interview. The campus interview is fundamentally a selling situation with an accompanying weeding out of unsuitable candidates. It does little good to accurately assess a candidate, to determine that he or she is an excellent prospect for the company, but, at the same time, fail to interest the individual. Clearly, the recruiting interview is one in which the interviewer must interest the desired student in coming to the company. On the other hand, the recruiter cannot indiscriminately make a job offer or invitation to a company location. Thus the campus interview places unusual demands on the interviewer by the duality of the role. Many executives are effective in selling the firm and in assessing candidates, but few are good at performing both tasks simultaneously.

A second problem of the campus interview is the time restriction placed upon the interviewer. Most campus interviews are scheduled for twenty- or thirty-minute intervals, and of that time, only fifteen to twenty minutes are available for evaluating the student—the remaining time being required for the introduction, selling, and the like. In contrast, the evaluation model described in this book requires forty-five minutes or more for the young college graduate. In view of the time limitation, the interviewer must set realistic expectations with regard to what he or she attempts to learn about the candidate.

The third feature of the campus interview that distinguishes it from the typical evaluation interview is the fatigue factor and the pressure placed upon the interviewer. It is not unusual for a campus interviewer to see fifteen or twenty students in one day. While there is a break for lunch, most campus interviewers experience a complete lack of sensitivity after seeing seven or eight students. It is difficult for the interviewer to maintain interest, enthusiasm, and attention for extended periods of time. Consequently, any approach to campus interviewing must take into account the numbness that will occur if many students are interviewed. The campus interview must be designed to permit the interviewer time to relax during the interview so that alertness and perceptivity can be maintained.

The Campus Interview Model

The campus interview model, as shown in Figure 23, has been designed to take into account the issues already mentioned, namely: time pressure, fatigue and boredom, and the need to sell. It has been used extensively by a number of major corporations. The approach lends itself well to most campus interview situations and is recommended as a starting point for the formulation of each executive's method of interviewing on campus. Particular company needs may occasionally require modification of the model, but the basic approach works well for most situations and individual personality styles.

Part 1—Opening Comments

Because the time for the campus interview is limited, it usually is neither wise nor necessary to spend much time in attempting to establish rapport with the student. As is true

FIGURE 23.   Model for conduct of campus interview.

Interview Segment		Approximate Time Allotted
Part 1	Opening Comments Establish rapport	3 minutes
Part 2	Specific Facts	2 minutes
Part 3	Assessment Section Make-or-break questions Broad-brush/self-appraisal questions	12 minutes
Part 4	Selling Section What is applicant looking for in company? Questions student has about company	12 minutes
Part 5	Closing Section Next steps	1 minute

for the evaluation interview, the most important factor in establishing rapport is for the interviewer to be natural; warmth, openness, and spontaneity also help. The interviewer should remember that the student may be more at ease than the interviewer. It could be that the student has already completed twenty interviews with other interviewers. Moreover, interviewers should recognize that the student is also interviewing them, so the usual social remarks can be kept minimal. After a few opening comments, the interviewer should plunge directly into the interview.

In view of the pressure to cover a reasonable amount of ground in a short period of time, it is quite important that the interviewer maintain adequate control over the interview. Control, however, does not mean dominating the interview but rather having a firm hand on what is being discussed at specific points during the interview.

Students are often inclined to disrupt control by asking questions at a time when the interviewer is trying to obtain certain data. To discourage interruptions and to minimize the likelihood of losing control of the interview, the interviewer can structure the discussion at the outset. Because of the added importance of control in this tightly scheduled situation, a somewhat modified structuring statement may be used.

INTERVIEWER: I know that in our meeting today we are both attempting to learn a little bit about what we can offer one another. We certainly would like to learn about your background and interests, and I know you are interested in learning about what our company has to offer. So let's divide the time up here a bit. I'd like to spend the first half of the interview getting acquainted with you, and then we'll turn it around and let you ask me about us.

The time allotted for the opening portion of the interview should be quite brief—no more than two or three minutes.

Part 2—Specific Facts

In each campus interview, it is important for most organizations that certain specific information be gathered. For at least two reasons, this fact-gathering should not be left until the end of the interview.

If you wait until the end of the interview, the likelihood of not recording the facts is great. It is often a temptation to say to yourself that you will write them down "at the end of the day." However, fatigue and the inability to remember one student from the other precludes this approach as an effective way of recalling data. Thus, critical factual data should be obtained at the very outset of the interview and immediately recorded.

It is important to gather certain facts at the beginning since occasionally those data will dictate how the interview will be conducted. You might find out, for example, that the student is not an applicant for full-time employment, but is simply looking for summer work; or you may find that certain students are completely unqualified and it may not be necessary to continue the interview, saving both the student's time and your own.

For most campus interviews, there are at least four items that are often helpful to be discussed at the beginning of the interview. Each company may have its own list of such items and they, of course, should be added to the following.

Get a transcript request signed. A written request is usually required if it is desired to obtain the student's transcript from the campus registrar. A sample form is shown in Appendix E. While the student is signing the form and filling out his or her address, several other questions can be asked.

Check to be certain that the address and telephone number indicated on the résumé are current. Students move frequently from the time they make out their résumé (which may well have been in the beginning of the school year) and if you do not have a current address, delays will occur in correspondence.

Check to see that the student is graduating when expected. As was mentioned, many students may be planning on graduating a semester later and are only looking for summer employment. Even if the student will not be graduating, it might be desirable to continue with the interview, assess the student, and try to sell him or her on your company. You also can suggest that the student talk with one of your company recruiters who may be visiting the campus closer to the time of graduation.

It is also worthwhile to inquire as to whether or not the applicant has had other contact with personnel from your company—particularly if your company has several interviewers on campus. Such questioning can help avoid having the student receive several different pieces of correspondence from your company's college placement office.

Part 3—Assessment Section

This assessment segment of the interview is designed to help the interviewer gain a better understanding of the applicant. Keeping in mind the problems of time and pressure, the interviewer must set realistic goals in terms of how comprehensive an assessment can actually be made. To try to make hire, not-hire decisions under the usual campus conditions is entirely unrealistic. What is realistic? Given the conditions available, the interviewer ought to try and achieve the answer to this question, "If this candidate walked into my office, would he or she be the kind of person I would say I was reasonably proud to have recruited?" In other words, in a campus interview, the interviewer should determine the candidate's past record of performance, such as grades and achievements, and examine observable characteristics that can rather easily be assessed in the face-to-face discussion. Some of these are

- ☐ How the applicant communicates.
- ☐ Extent of initiative-taking or self-starting ability.
- ☐ How applicant thinks. Organized? Scattered? Too much focus on detail?
- ☐ Degree of social perceptivity (often can be gleaned from student's perception of expectations regarding length of responses to questions, knowing when to talk and when to listen, and appropriateness of appearance and dress).
- ☐ Extent of self-assurance and poise.
- ☐ Extent to which the necessary technical background was acquired.

To attempt to make assessments in these areas is to set a realistic goal. To obtain a more perceptive analysis is not likely—at least not without the interviewer becoming a candidate for psychotherapy.

To achieve this objective, the assessment segment of the interview can be divided into two parts—a make-or-break portion and a self-appraisal section.

Make or Break Questions Few things can be more frustrating to the campus interviewer than to spend thirty minutes with a student only to find out that he really was not interested in the company and is planning to go to graduate school; he only wanted to "hear about the opportunities in your industry." Immediately after the opening comments, the interviewer should introduce questions about make-or-break items for which there must be agreement if the candidate is to be considered further. For example, for most sales positions the candidate must have a valid driver's license. Lacking the license, the employee could not make customer calls. For some companies, willingness to relocate might be a crucial item, or willingness to travel, or a particular skill, such as knowledge of fusion physics. If such factors exist as fundamental requirements for hiring, it is prudent to talk about them at the outset. Most students also appreciate learning whether or not there is a "match," particularly if it saves them from needlessly investing their time. Of course, when recruiters are interviewing for many different departments or jobs, the make-or-break items may not need to be mentioned.

Here is one way of introducing make-or-break items.

INTERVIEWER: Before we get into the interview, there are a couple of matters we should touch on—just to make sure we're in the same ball park as far as your qualifications for the marketing position are concerned. First of all, the jobs that I'm interviewing for require considerable overnight travel. Is that any problem for you?

APPLICANT: I don't mind a little travel.

INTERVIEWER: Well, in this job you will be away, on the average, four and sometimes five nights a week. Is that excessive for you?

APPLICANT: Oh, I don't think I'd want that. I'm really not interested in having to be away that much. I'm interested in taking some evening graduate courses.

INTERVIEWER: As I say, this job would require fairly extensive travel; sometimes it could be less than I said, but often-times it could be quite prolonged, so I doubt very much that this is a job that's going to meet your needs.

APPLICANT: Well, thank you very much for telling me about the traveling, because I don't think I would be very interested.

If no make-or-break factors seem pertinent to the job, the interviewer can skip this portion of the interview and go on to a more qualitative appraisal.

Broad Brush and Self-Appraisal Questions Before discussing the specific techniques to be employed in this section of the campus interview, it may be helpful to review the limitations imposed by the recruiting interview. First there is the question of depth of the assessment. There are certain inputs that the interviewer realistically can expect to glean from the campus interview—verbal ability, confidence level, poise, and the like. But analysis of motivation patterns and assessment of personality strengths and limitations are difficult, if not impossible, during the campus interview. The interviewer should also recognize that much of the needed factual data is already available to him through application blanks, college transcripts, or résumés, and there is no point in eliciting this same information during the interview. Consequently, the interview should be focused to help the manager judge whether or not this is the kind of person who can work effectively in the organization.

A second factor to be considered about the assessment portion is the interviewer's need for time to sit back, relax, and take notes about how the applicant behaves. To accomplish this and at the same time obtain some assessment of the candidate, the interviewer might ask the student a number of broad questions that force the applicant to carry the burden of responsibility for the dialog. These should be questions that require the applicant to verbalize freely, organize thoughts, communicate well, and think aloud. The ideal questions are those sufficiently broad in scope that they require the applicants to analyze their own thoughts. For example:

- □ "What long-term satisfactions do you expect to derive from a career in the business world?"
- □ "How do you evaluate your college career as a preparation for your future?"
- □ "What are your thoughts about __(finance, accounting, history)__ that you think would sustain your interest and motivation in the years ahead?"

For each student, the interviewer should be prepared to ask two or three of these broad questions. Once a broad-brush question is asked, the interviewer can sit back, and observe the student. It is at this point that the interviewer can begin to make some judgments as to whether or not the student has some of the basic qualities the company is seeking. In this way the interviewer is also able to preserve his mental and physical well-being.

A problem that can occur if the interviewer asks all of the candidates the same questions is that the students will tell their friends the questions asked, and as the day goes on, each applicant will appear more and more knowledgeable or fluent. To minimize this possibility, the interviewer should prepare a list of approximately twelve broad-brush questions. A long list of such questions is given in Appendix A. These questions can be written on a small card and kept on the desk in front of the interviewer. For the first student interviewed, the interviewer will ask broad-brush questions 1 and 2; for the second student, questions 3 and 4; the third student, questions 5 and 6; and so on. In this way, each of the first six students is asked different questions. The process then is repeated for the next six students. This procedure helps ensure that all of the students come equally unprepared for the questions.

While listening to the responses of students, the interviewer should be recording observations about their behavior and qualifications.

Part 4—Selling Section

Many campus interviewers have limited success in selling or interesting students in their companies because they do not adequately respond to the needs of the students. Instead, they are likely to recite a litany of the advantages of working for their company. But when these advantages are compared, in the eyes of the student, with the advantages offered by other companies, few organizations can distinguish themselves by exceptional benefits or opportunities. Thus much of the time spent in trying to interest the student has little impact and, from the student's point of view, may even seem completely irrelevant.

One approach that helps the campus interviewer relate the company to the needs of the student is simply to ask the student what he or she is looking for. Once an answer is given, the interviewer can point out to the candidate how the company might fulfill the student's particular desires. Here is an example of how the selling section of the interview might be initiated.

INTERVIEWER: I am sure that there are certain things you are looking for as you take these interviews with various companies—features that help you to evaluate prospective employers. What are some of the elements that, to your mind, would make a company or an employment situation attractive to you?

APPLICANT: Well, I guess one thing I'm looking for is an opportunity to get my feet wet in a fairly responsible position quite soon. I feel I'm a little more mature than many of those graduating with me—having worked two years before starting school. I'd like a job where I can step in and really show what I can do. I don't think I'm interested in getting involved with a long training program, but I'd like a job where I could be given a little rope. And, I guess, the other major thing I'm looking for is that I would like to locate near a metropolitan area where I could continue my schooling in the evening. I want to work toward my M.B.A., so I wouldn't want to be in a situation where I had to travel a lot or where I wouldn't be near a graduate school.

INTERVIEWER: Well, the goals you've set for yourself certainly make a lot of sense and I think you'll be very excited
and interested in the kind of responsibility you would be
getting at XYZ Company. I think, too, I can assure you
that going on the graduate school would present no problem in our organization. Let me tell you about. . . .

If, for some reason, the student is unable to delineate
specific wants, it may be helpful for the interviewer to be
aware of some generalized findings about current job expectations as expressed by young college graduates. They seem
to be saying that they are looking for a participative company
climate or style, meaningful work, and a job that will provide
a sense of achievement. A recruiter who can specifically describe how these objectives can be attained in his company
will usually have little difficulty in stimulating student interest. To help the interviewer better understand what is on the
minds of most students, a list of the most frequently asked
questions in shown in Figure 24.

Once the interviewer has ascertained the applicant's
needs and has shown the applicant how these desires can be
fulfilled within the organization, it is then appropriate to
inquire about any questions the applicant may have. The
nature of the applicant's questions provides clues for assessing the applicant's desires and motivations, as well as avenues
for selling the applicant.

A key point in responding to the applicant's questions is to
be frank and honest. If the applicant raises a question about
which you do not have an answer, do not bluff. The interviewer
will come across as a much more effective company representative if seen as being straightforward and open.

Instead of bluffing or making generalized comments, it is
far better to indicate, "I don't know the exact answer to that,
but I will be pleased to find out for you and let you know."
This also provides a great opportunity for additional contact
with the student.

Obviously, the more you can know about the company, its
operations, and opportunities, the better. On the other hand,
no student can expect you to know in-depth the answers to

FIGURE 24.   Frequent student inquiries.

1. What is involved in the training program?
2. Can I progress at my own pace or is it structured?
3. How much travel is usually expected?
4. How frequently do you relocate professional employees?
5. What is the average age of top management?
6. How much visibility is there with top management?
7. What is the typical career progression?
8. How many trainees are you looking for?
9. Does the company promote solely from within?
10. How much decision-making authority is given?
11. How much input does a new person have on geographic location?
12. Is this position more analytical or more people-oriented?
13. What is your policy on tuition reimbursement?
14. Is graduate work encouraged during the training period?
15. How often are performance reviews given?
16. How soon after graduation would I expect to report to work?
17. What is the average time to become an officer?
18. What is the usual routine of a _____ like?
19. How much independence is allowed in dress and appearance?

all the questions that can be raised. In answering the questions which you know about, the interviewer is given a great opportunity to show enthusiasm for the company and the advantage of working there.

It should also be mentioned that the selling portion provides additional opportunity for evaluation. Students are definitely revealing something about themselves as they talk about their interests and needs.

Part 5—Closing Section

The essential point in the closing section is to indicate to the student the next step in the employment procedure. The student should be told, for example, whether or not the next step will be an invitation to visit a company location, an offering letter, or whatever. The applicant also should be told the approximate length of time that will lapse between the interview and the next communication from the company.

Companies vary greatly in their procedures for post-interview visits or job offers, but it should be clear that speed and promptness are extremely important. One reason prompt action is so significant is that it represents a concrete way of showing that the company is interested in the applicant.

A survey was made of 130 chemical and mechanical engineers who were recruited for a major chemical company. Once the recruits were on board, they were interviewed to determine why they accepted the company's job offer. The results are summarized here.

Reason Given	Percent
The company seemed personally interested in me	42
Advancement opportunities seemed good	27
The jobs seemed challenging or interesting	18
Reputation of the company	10
Miscellaneous	3

In examining what the respondents meant by "the company seemed personally interested in me," the analysis revealed such statements as:

I received my offering letter three days after my visit to the plant. It seemed that the company really wanted me.

When I was at the plant, the plant personnel were interested in what I wanted to do and the kinds of jobs I wanted to get involved in—they just didn't try to sell me.

The evening after the recruiter interviewed me on campus, he phoned the dormitory and extended me a verbal offer of employment. It seemed to me that I must have created a very positive impression and that he wanted to be sure that he got me.

In essence, these students seem to be saying that the prompt action by the company was a significant factor in their decision to accept the employment offer. Such action is interpreted by many students as a concrete measure of the company's true interest in them. It really is important, therefore, that the campus interviewer outline the next steps in the employment procedure and tell the applicants when they will take place. The sooner these next steps are taken, the better.

The Home Office Interview (Second Interview)

The home office interview usually takes place after an invitation is extended during the campus visit or in a subsequent letter. Its purpose is twofold: to make a hire, not-hire decision about the candidate and to sell the candidate on the desirability of accepting an offer with the company. The assessment procedures outlined in this book are ideally suited to this final interview. However, in most companies, special problems occur when the young candidates arrive at the doorstep. They are subject to the "beauty parade."

The approach used for the second interviews is the procedure described in Chapter 9, called the evaluation model, a comprehensive interview that requires at least forty-five to fifty minutes. However, the thoroughness of the interview makes it unnecessary to run candidates through more than two such interviews; that amounts to overkill. The thorough, in-depth evaluation interview also militates against the "beauty parade"—a process in which the candidate is interviewed by five or six executives, each of whom is expected to evaluate the candidate and/or sell him or her on the company. The applicant is whisked from one manager to the next for a series of thirty-minute interviews, including, perhaps, a luncheon interview with one of the younger members of the staff. By the end of the day, the applicant has literally been through a wringer.

Problems of the Beauty Parade

Before discussing the positive steps that can be taken to make the secondary interview effective, it may be worthwhile to first examine some of the problems inherent in use of the beauty parade approach. There is serious question that thirty-minute interviews are of much value, except for the most superficial of observations. There isn't even thirty minutes for evaluation when one considers the time invested in introductions, small talk, and explanation about career opportunities in the interviewer's area of operation.

A second problem with the beauty parade approach is that it diminishes the ability of the company to make accurate predictions about job performance. An interviewing team may arrive at erroneous conclusions because they disagree about superficial issues. This is because they do not all interview the same person; during the course of a day of interviewing, the applicant changes in several ways. The manager who interviews the candidate at 4:30 P.M. sees quite a different individual than the one with whom a breakfast interview was held at the airport.

One way in which applicants change is that they become sophisticated about the interview; that is, they begin to learn the right things to say. As students proceed from one interviewer to the next, they learn from comments made, both overt and subtle, the kinds of reactions and responses the interviewers are looking for. They learn which values are prized in the company, what will be expected of them on the job, and which answers result in positive responses from the interviewers.

After having made several home office visits, most students become adept in interview-taking. Unless company interviewers make frequent use of the self-appraisal techniques, they will be "snowed" by the extraordinary appropriateness of the candidate's responses.

A second change, and one that somewhat offsets the sophistication advantage, is fatigue. As the day wears on, students are likely to lose some of their bounce and enthusiasm. Students often report that after four or five interviews, each covering about the same ground, they get bored with the process. Near the end of the day, the student is more interested in getting it done than in exploring employment opportunities. Thus, the candidate appears to have less interest in the job or in the company. This may be especially true of the most qualified candidate who may already have obtained two or three job offers from competitors. The candidates' physical appearance also becomes rumpled as the day wears on.

A third problem is that the attitudes and opinions of the poorer interviewers dilute the judgments of those who are more skillful. Let's look at a typical situation.

Candidate A is aggressive, bright, hard-driving, but frank and outspoken. The applicant has a good record of accomplishment but had been involved in a scrape with the dean's office.

Let us use the hypothetical situation summarized in Figure 25. Assume that six persons are to interview Candidate A. Assume further that interviewers number 2 and number 4 are astute in evaluating others.

Interviewer 1, a relatively unskillful assessor of others, decides to turn down the candidate. This interviewer sees the candidate as something of a rabble-rouser whose outspokenness is going to rub too many people the wrong way. The interviewer thinks that the candidate will not be able to get the kind of cooperation from others that the job will demand. Interviewers 3, 5, and 6 evaluate the candidate in much the same way. Interviewer 2 observes the same flaws in the candidate's behavior as do Interviewers 1, 3, 5, and 6, but also recognizes that the candidate is a highly competent individual whose strengths more than offset some of the shortcomings. Interviewer 2 votes to hire. Interviewer 4, who is

FIGURE 25.   *Dilutions of evaluations as function of the beauty parade.*

Candidate	Interviewers' Reactions						Group Consensus
	1	2	3	4	5	6	
A	No	Yes	No	Yes	No	No	No
B	Yes	Yes	Yes	Yes	Yes	Yes	Yes

also perceptive, evaluates the candidate in much the same way as Interviewer 2. Now all opinions are combined. In some companies, interviewers write their assessment and submit it to the personnel department; in others, the interviewers meet to arrive at some consensus. Regardless of the method, Candidate A is not likely to be given an offer.

Now let us look at Candidate B. This person is reasonably intelligent, communicates well, seems pleasant, and has a good record (no scrapes with the dean's office). Candidate B did not appear opinionated or outspoken in the interview. Interviewer 1 evaluates the candidate as good; no problems were observed, so the vote is yes. The remaining interviewers also see the candidate as satisfactory. No one sees any significant flaws in this applicant's background; so Candidate B is given an offer.

Candidate B certainly should be extended an offer. The applicant is good but not outstanding. However, Candidate A may well have been the superior candidate. Because the applicant is a strong individual who is more self-confident, aggressive, and forceful, the shortcomings are evident, even to the poor assessor. Self-assured applicants will openly tell you some of their shortcomings because they feel no need to hide them; they are confident of their abilities.

Frequently, inexperienced interviewers become unduly upset by shortcomings, particularly if they are identified early in the interview. They find it difficult to focus on the candidate's strengths and to determine how these assets might more than offset the shortcomings.

Another problem of the beauty parade is that it often alienates the applicants rather than helping them to develop positive attitudes toward the company. A daylong series of interviews, whether designed to assess or sell, probably does not represent the most effective use of time.

The Twosome Approach

One way to cope with problems of the beauty parade is to reduce the number of interviews to which the applicant is exposed. This can be accomplished by use of group interviewers, that is, having more than one person simultaneously interview the candidate. In working with a wide range of clients, I have experimented with combinations of two-on-one, three-on-one, and four-on-one. While I am not yet convinced that three-on-one and four-on-one cannot be made to work effectively, efforts thus far have not been successful. Good results, however, have been obtained with the two-on-one method. The results are not only good, but are significantly superior to the predictive accuracy obtained by the traditional one-on-one method of interviewing.

A demonstration of the effectiveness of the twosome approach grew out of the chemical company research project mentioned previously. Two interviewing teams evaluated the staff of a newly acquired firm. Team A was trained in use of the evaluation model and employed the twosome method to evaluate twenty-five of the fifty-four candidates interviewed. Team B members interviewed singly, using whatever method seemed most satisfactory to each interviewer.

To arrive at their evaluations, Team A members combined the respective ratings of each pair to form a composite evaluation. Team B members, on the other hand, combined the individual judgments to form their composite assessment.

Top management of the acquired firm was asked to rate its executives in rank order in terms of their qualifications for their current management assignments. Data about salary progression were also obtained.

The team evaluations were then correlated with top management's evaluations. The results in Figure 26 show clearly that there is a statistically significant difference between levels of correlations obtained by Team A raters, who used the

FIGURE 26.   *Comparison of twosome and single methods of interviewing, with Team A using twosome method.*

Interview Method	Team	Correlations with Performance Ratings	
Twosome	A	Managerial Rating	.52
		Salary Progress	.39
Single	B	Managerial Rating	.26
		Salary Progress	.18

twosome approach, and those scored by Team B raters, who used individual interviews.

A possible explanation of the superior assessment performance of Team A could be that the team was composed of individuals more talented in evaluating others than was true of Team B. To check this hypothesis, the same teams evaluated an additional forty individuals in the acquired company. This time, the persons to be evaluated were at lower levels in the company. On this round of assessments, the two teams reversed procedures, Team B using the pair method and Team A, the individual method. As shown in Figure 27, the team using the twosome approach was able to predict job success better than the team using the individual method.

How to Make the Twosome Approach Work

When the idea is proposed that two persons simultaneously interview one candidate, the usual reaction from most executives is that such an approach would be too threatening, the applicant would feel "under the gun" and become uneasy or defensive. This is not the case, however, if the interview is properly structured. The factor that creates tension in multiple interviews is the problem the interviewee has in relating to two or more people simultaneously. This problem can be avoided by structuring the interview so only one interviewer of the pair is interviewing at any given time. This does not mean a back-and-forth questioning with each interviewer alternately addressing the applicant. Instead, one of the partners (after both participate in the social amenities) starts off the interview process by covering all the areas in the

FIGURE 27.   Comparison of twosome and single methods of interviewing, with Team B using twosome method.

Interview Method	Team	Correlations with Performance Ratings	
Twosome	B	Managerial Rating	.46
		Salary Progress	.32
Single	A	Managerial Rating	.24
		Salary Progress	.23

interview plan. This is accomplished by using the evaluation model, without interruption by the other member of the interviewing team.

It is helpful if the two interviewers sit at some distance from each other, so the candidate does not have to try to maintain eye contact with both. It should be made clear that the applicant should focus on only one of the interviewers.

When the first interviewer has completed all steps in the interview plan, the interview is turned over to the partner. This individual does not follow an interview plan but, instead, inquires about specific technical skills and factual information, or clarifies topics brought up earlier. The partner in the second part of the twosome approach may also reexplore some areas already discussed. However, this is not recommended unless it is essential to obtain additional information in the area in question. The portion of time used by the second interviewer usually is from ten to fifteen minutes; the first interviewer spends approximately forty-five minutes. Thus, most two-on-one interviews require approximately an hour to complete.

For the twosome approach to be effective, it must be made clear to the applicant how the interview will be conducted. Unless the interviewers' procedures are discussed, it will seem peculiar that only one person is talking; the candidate might feel sorry for the partner who seems left out and try to involve the quiet interviewer in the discussion. It is important, therefore, at the outset, to explain the interview structure and to provide some rationale for the format. The following statement works well:

> In order to cut down on the number of different interviews you'll have to go through today, we would like to interview you together. But, since it might be difficult to talk with two of us at the same time, suppose I begin, and when I'm finished, _____ will take over. How would that be?

Most applicants will feel no more ill at ease than in the one-on-one interview. Many indicate they find it comfortable and stimulating. This was substantiated in the study described earlier. As the reader may recall, forty candidates were interviewed by two teams of interviewers. One team used the twosome approach, and the other, the one-on-one interview. When the candidates completed an interview, each was asked to indicate the degree of discomfort experienced in each interview. They were asked to rate the tension experienced on a scale of one to nine. The average degree of tension reported by those interviewed by the one-at-a-time method was 4.2 and by the twosome approach, 4.8. These differences are not statistically significant.

Companies that use the dual-interviewer system are able to reduce by almost half the amount of time they spend in interviews. If the candidate is visiting the plant or home office for a day, this allows ample time for other activities that might successfully interest the candidate in the company.

It is interesting to note, too, that almost every client who has experimented with the two-on-one interviews has remained with the procedure. The twosome approach has produced more accurate predictions.

Advantages of the Twosome Approach

One way in which the twosome approach helps increase accuracy in hiring decisions is that two persons witness the same event simultaneously. These concurrent observations, when merged, produce a significantly more accurate prediction than two independent observations combined.

What one interviewer misses, the other observes. Also, in the discussion and preparation of the balance sheet at the termination of the interview, there is opportunity to share perceptions and more properly determine the appropriate weight or emphasis to be placed on the identified characteristics of the candidate. For example, one interviewer may have confirmed the hypothesis in his or her notes that the candidate is wishy-washy and fails to take firm positions. The second interviewer, however, may remind the first of an instance during the interview when the applicant strongly defended a particular point. Thus, together they may agree to assign less weight to this factor than was previously thought appropriate.

The twosome approach also permits one interviewer to study the applicant while the other is busy conducting the interview. Thus, the silent interviewer has the opportunity to make many observed hypotheses that may escape his or her partner. When it is the observer's turn to take over the interview, that person can follow up on hunches and unresolved questions that the other interviewer may have overlooked or for some reason decided not to pursue.

Another advantage of the twosome approach is that it allows interviewers of diverse skills and backgrounds to combine observations and judgments. A practical combination, for instance, is an interviewer who is particularly effective at evaluating intellect, motivation, and personality teamed with a technological expert who can evaluate the candidate's knowledge and experience. In this combination, the personnel specialist usually interviews first, using the evaluation model, and the technological expert follows, asking specific technical questions.

Some companies have found the twosome approach helpful when a large number of persons want to make judgments about the applicant, but time does not permit individual interviews. While an applicant is interviewed in the standard two-on-one format, others, seated in the background, can observe and make notes on the basis of the interview being conducted in front of them. If the group is not too large (fewer than six or seven), a conference discussion can follow the interview with a balance sheet developed from the consensus of the entire group.

Use of Interview Rating Forms

It is important not to complicate the recruiting process by requiring interviewers to complete complex evaluation sheets or forms. On the other hand, there obviously is a need for the interviewers to record their impressions at the conclusion of each interview. Such records are also essential if the organization is interested in evaluating tte effectiveness of its recruiting effort. Thus, some evaluation format is needed. Unfortunately, in an effort to develop easy-to-complete evaluation forms, most organizations lean heavily on the checklist approach, at least for a portion of the form. An example of this type if shown in Figure 28.

Parts of this form clearly are helpful and deserve the space allotted to them. For instance, the section on "Interviewer's Recommendations" is efficient and helpful. On the other hand, serious objection must be taken to use of the checklist in which the interviewer is asked to indicate an evaluation of initiative, maturity, and like qualities.

Problems with Checklists

There are a number of problems with checklists that make them inappropriate for use as interview evaluation forms. There is the assumption that the factors listed account for success at work. Of course, there can be no argument that these skills or qualities are desirable. The question is, are they valid predictors of success? In two studies conducted by Drake-Beam and Associates Inc., ratings made on client evaluation forms from campus interviews were correlated with ratings of subsequent job performance on the basis of the same characteristics. There was almost no significant correlation between the trait qualities on the form (factors similar to those indicated in Figure 28) and ratings on these same factors after a year's observation of job performance. The only factor for which there was a slightly significant, positive relationship was appearance—manner of dress and neatness.

The evaluation of specific personality qualities or traits contributes little to accurate prediction of job success. There may be other, far more significant factors that explain the individual's ability to perform successfully in a given job. For instance, a candidate may not show much evidence of initiative but is successful at work because of a conscientious, persistent approach that enables the person to accomplish more than many peers.

Because a candidate displays a certain characteristic is no guarantee that it is good or desirable; it all depends on the other elements in the individual's makeup. One may find that the applicant takes initiative, but if the individual is also highly egotistical, the initiatives will be self-serving and possibly even anti-company.

Another problem with use of rating scales on interview

FIGURE 28.   *Example of trait checklist interview form.*

Interview Evaluation	**Instructions**—Complete this form for each applicant interviewed, whether or not he or she is being recommended by you. Attach this form in front of other material pertaining to the applicant (i.e. application, résumé, etc.). Return all campus interview information to College Relations.

Last Name	First Name	Address

College	Degree	Date of Degree	Grade Point Average

		Poor	Average	Excellent
Appearance	(Neatness, Personal Habits, Manners)	Poor		Excellent
Communication	(Verbal Expression, Organization)	Poor		Superior
Maturity	(Responsible, Reasonable, Aspirations)	Immature		Very Mature
Initiative	(Self-reliant, Industrious, Motivated)	Lazy		Vigorous
Leadership	(Participation in Activities, Offices Held)	Inactive		Very Active
Technical	(Comprehension, Theory)	Poor		Excellent
Overall Evaluation	(Consider all of above factors)	Poor		Superior

Comment On Evaluation (Include Honorary Societies)

Interviewer's Recommendations
☐ Reject
Invite For:
☐ Eng. Program
☐ Mfg. Program
☐ Graduate Study Program
☐ Research Training Program

☐ Computer Sales & Systems Program
☐ Financial Mgmt. Career Program
☐ Mgt. Info. Systems Career Program
☐ Operations Research Career Program
☐ Materials Mgmt. Development Program

☐ Marketing Program
☐ Personnel Mgmt. Development Program
☐ Direct Hire Referral
☐ Other (Specify)

Specific Vocational Interests Expressed By Applicant	Applicable Work or Military Experience

Locations To Which Applicant Should Be Referred	Application
	☐ Attached ☐ Send to ☐ Not
	☐ Given to Applicant Applicant Required
	Recruiter's Name (Please Print) Facility-Ext Date

evaluation forms is the implication that all the factors checked were observed equally well. For example, the interviewer's rating on "appearance" may result from far more complete observation than the rating on "maturity," which may have been derived from a fleeting and superficial "gut reaction." And yet, the credence given to each scale is almost equal.

The presence of factors on the rating form implies that the interviewer should be making observations on each of the factors and that it is realistic to do so. Consequently, ratings are frequently checked off so that the form looks "properly" completed. If for some reason the interviewer did not learn anything about a particular characteristic, a rating is usually made on a "best guess" basis, if only to avoid being judged as a poor assessor.

A more meaningful format for recording information about a campus interview is shown in Figure 29. Notice here how the interviewer is asked to comment only about realistically observable issues. And, since the spaces are completely open, only actually observed behavior is apt to be recorded. An even more ideal form might simply provide a large open space for "Comments and Reactions."

The Sell Portion of the Student's Visit

Use of the twosome approach can substantially reduce the time spent in evaluation interviewing. This time can be put to good use in selling the student.

An effective approach to selling students is to provide opportunity for them to build an identity with the company. One way to accomplish this is to allow the student to participate in some of the activities and situations he or she would encounter as an employee. For example, a large oil company uses the morning of the visit for assessment interviews and in the afternoon assigns the student to a young employee recruited a year or two earlier, so that the student can accompany the employee as he performs his afternoon tasks. The student attends meetings, helps write reports, talks with the other managers, questions the employee. The student is allowed to spend as little or as much time with the employee as he or she likes.

FIGURE 29.   *Example of semistructured campus interview form.*

INITIAL INTERVIEW REPORT	RECRUITING YEAR 19 ⎪ 19	Interview Date
Name of Candidate	Home Address and Phone No.	

Campus Address and Phone No.

School	Degree/Major	Graduation Date

Candidate's Geographic Preference or Limitations

	ASSESSMENT OF INDIVIDUAL QUALIFICATIONS (NOTES AND COMMENTS ABOUT OBSERVATIONS)
Accomplishments and Work Experiences	
Interpersonal Skills	
Intellectual Abilities	
Direction and Interests	

Summary Comments and Reactions

Overall, I would rate this candidate as

Below Average	Aver. to Below Aver.	Average	Aver. to Above Aver.	Above Average

Referral Recommendation: (check one)   [ ] Refer
[ ] Reject

Interviewer	Title	Unit	Date

The advantages of this work-along-with-me approach are numerous. As the student accompanies the employee on rounds, he or she is naturally introduced to the company employees. During the course of the afternoon, the applicant often feels as though already on board. Moreover, students often report that the key factor that attracted them to this particular oil company was that they could visualize exactly what they would be doing. The offering letters they received did not represent abstract employment situations but rather called to mind specific people, work tasks, and company environment.

It is possible that the work-along procedure might be difficult or even impossible to implement in certain job situations—for example, when security measures prohibit such tours—but many companies have effectively adopted it in sales offices, research laboratories, and plant locations.

It is recommended that companies give consideration to ways of selling students other than through a series of interviews. Work-along procedures, tours, discussion meetings with last year's graduates, and a give-and-take conversation with the company president all have proved effective for recruiting. It is usually expensive to bring students for these visits, and if the candidate is evaluated as good, at least as much care should be given to the sell portion of the day as is given to the assessment.

Summary

The manager who is hiring college seniors may engage in two types of interviews—one on the college campus and the other at the home office. The model for the conduct of a campus interview provides for the fact that the campus interview is fundamentally a selling interview with limited assessment goals. The interviewer establishes rapport simply by being natural and structures the roles in the interview by telling the candidate there will be time to ask questions later. The manager begins the assessment section with make-or-break questions, learning immediately if the student possesses the fundamental requirements for hiring such as willingness to travel. If the candidate is not disqualified, the interviewer continues the assessment with self-appraisal questions designed to allow time to record observations and formulate hypotheses about the behavior and qualifications of the candidate. In the selling section of the interview, one approach that helps the campus interviewer relate remarks about the company to the interests of the student is to ask what the student is seeking. Closing the interview, the manager should tell the student the next step in the employment procedure.

The purpose of the home office interview is to make a hire, not-hire decision about the candidate and to sell the desirability of accepting an offer with the company. An approach that allows for sales time and yet permits accurate hire, not-hire decisions is the use of dual interviewers. Companies using the twosome approach reduce by half the amount of time spent in interviews, and the candidate has time to participate in selling activities such as accompanying a young employee through the routine for the afternoon.

CHAPTER 15

Interviewing and Fair Employment Practices

This is an important subject for interviewers, because about 70 percent of discrimination complaints arising out of compliance legislation have occurred as a result of the interviewing process.

Many interviewers are uncertain about the requirements of Equal Employment Opportunity (EEO) regulations, so they feel constrained in efforts to identify the most suitable candidate for a job. However, through use of the hypothesis method, interviewers can learn enough about the candidate to determine an applicant's qualifications.

The groups most affected by EEO regulations are:

□ Women
□ Vietnam-era veterans (separated after August 5, 1964)
□ Forty- to sixty-five-year-olds
□ Minorities (Black, Oriental, American Indian, or Spanish-surnamed American)
□ The handicapped

An Overview—What Are the Regulations?

The interviewer should understand that no question *per se* is really illegal. The problem in interviewing is that asking certain questions could make the interviewer vulnerable to the charge of discrimination. If the interviewer inquires about age, for example, and subsequently a forty-five-year-old applicant does not receive a job offer, the candidate could claim that you failed to hire because of age. It would then be incumbent upon the interviewer to prove that age was not a factor in the not-hire decision.

Basically, the federal laws state that decisions about employment cannot be made on the basis of sex, race, color, age, religion, national origin, or handicap. There are, of course, exceptions to these rules in situations which the EEO Commission calls bona fide occupational qualifications (BFOQs). If you were hiring a fashion model, for example, you would set age and sex requirements and reject those not meeting your criteria.

It should be noted, too, that unintentional discrimination is just as illegal as intentional discrimination. It is no protection in a suit against your company to say you "didn't know" that the information you solicited was discriminatory. The burden of proof of innocence is on the one doing the hiring. Even apparently innocent questions, asked in good faith, can leave the company open to costly and time-consuming litigation.

It should be recognized, too, that each state has its own laws on discrimination, so organizations should obtain copies of these regulations from their state Human Rights Commission.

Volunteered Information

Sometimes, without prompting from the interviewer, applicants volunteer information that could provide the basis for a charge of discrimination in hiring. A female applicant, for example, may reveal that she is planning to be married next month. In such a case, the interviewer should refrain from asking anything further about plans for a family or relocation plans but, instead, should stop the applicant from volunteering additional information on the topic. The interviewer may make statements such as, "I would appreciate your not saying anything further about your marriage status. It is our policy to hire only on the basis of your ability to do the job. We really don't need to know this information to judge your qualifications, so while I thank you for your openness, let's go on now to another topic."

Once illegal information is "out on the table" and you have attempted to stop the flow of such information, it would be wise to indicate in your notes that the candidate volunteered data about some particular point and the applicant was asked to refrain from further discussion about the topic.

The specific information should be kept with your records and not forwarded to the next interviewers.

Interviewers should recognize that attempts to be nondiscriminatory will not be lost on the applicant. Most will appreciate your effort to comply with the law. In fact, your statements could have a positive impact in making the company attractive to candidates.

What You Can and Cannot Ask

Many seemingly appropriate questions can get an interviewer into trouble with the EEOC. The following lists the major areas to be alert to, along with specific questions that should be avoided.

Sex

You cannot use sex as a basis for hiring, unless sex is a bona fide occupational requirement. Few companies have such jobs. Here are some often used sex-based reasons for not hiring a candidate—all of which could be the basis for a claim against the company for discriminatory hiring practices:

1. The job was traditionally restricted to members of the opposite sex.

2. The job involved travel or travel with members of the opposite sex.

3. The assumption that, because some members of one sex are unable or unwilling to do the job, other candidates of that sex are inappropriate choices. Examples are assuming that a female candidate is not suitable for a job as a miner or

firefighter, or that a male candidate is not appropriate for a secretarial position.

4. The job involves heavy physical labor, unpleasant work surroundings, overtime, isolated working situations, or late hours.

5. Preferences of customers, clients, co-workers, or employers.

6. Stereotyped characterizations of the sexes. Such stereotypes, for example, are that men are less capable of assembling intricate equipment, that women are less capable of aggressive salesmanship. The principle of nondiscrimination requires that individuals be considered on the basis of individual capabilities, not on the basis of any characteristics generally attributed to the group.

7. Unavailability of physical facilities, such as rest rooms for both sexes.

Other topics can be discriminatory to ask about. Because the potential for engaging in discriminatory practices with females is so great, the focus here is on the female candidate. Topics to avoid are

- Plans for raising a family.
- Marital plans; do not ask, "Are you married, single, divorced, separated, widowed?"
- Number and/or ages of dependents.
- Babysitting arrangements.
- Occupation of husband.
- Training or experience not expected of a male in a similar job, for example, typing ability for a chemist's job.
- Husband's reaction to travel away from home.

A more comprehensive view of the possibilities for even inadvertent discrimination can be gleaned from the items listed in Figure 30. This is a handout from the National Organization for Women (NOW). The reader should particularly note the last sentence.

Race or Color

Race is such an obvious area in which discrimination must be avoided, it will not be belabored here. The law states that

FIGURE 30.   Handout from NOW.

Have You Met With Sex Discrimination?

While Looking for a Job

Was the job advertised under a Help-Wanted column titled "male" or "female"?

Did the ad state or imply that a member of one sex was wanted for the position?

Were there different application forms for men and for women?

Did the employment agency/personnel office refer you to stereotyped "female" jobs if you were not seeking that type of job?

If a test was administered, was it related to the type of position you were seeking?

During a Job Interview

Did the interviewer ask you questions that would not ordinarily be asked of a man seeking a similar job?

Did the interviewer inquire about your children, marital status, marriage plans, plans to have children, birth control practices?

Did the interviewer state or imply any stereotyped myths about women employees, such as "they never stick with a job," "they are too emotional," "they can't get along with the men in a businesslike fashion"?

When Negotiating a Position

Did the employer offer you a lower salary than was advertised?

Are other positions still unfilled more commensurate with your education and experience?

Has the position been "downgraded" since the initial interview through changes in the number of employees to be supervised, changes in the person to whom you would report?

FIGURE 30. (continued)

Did They Fail to Hire You

Because the job involved travel, or travel with members of the opposite sex?

Because of unusual working hours, lack of rest room facilities, or weight lifting requirements?

Because you are pregnant, have small children?

Because the job has always been held by a man, or because the other employees indicated they would not work for a woman or with a woman?

Because a man applied who was almost as qualified?

In Your Present Job

Are there different seniority lines for men and women?

Do you receive less pay than a man doing a similar job?

Are raise and promotion policies different for men and women?

Are training programs, educational leaves restricted to men?

Are fringe benefits different for men and women— different pension plans, life insurance plans, health insurance plans, dates of optional or mandatory retirement?

Are the employee rules and regulations different for men and women?

Are there general patterns of discrimination in your place of employment, such as all-female departments, all women in certain types of jobs, no women in others?

Are disabilities caused or contributed to by pregnancy, miscarriage, or abortion exempted from disability benefits?

Are benefits conditioned on whether or not the employee is the "head of household" or "principal wage earner"?

IF YOU ANSWERED YES TO ANY OF THE ABOVE QUESTIONS, THEN YOU HAVE A BONA FIDE COMPLAINT AND MAY FILE A CHARGE AGAINST THE EMPLOYER.

you cannot discriminate against Blacks, Hispanics, Asians or Pacific Islanders, American Indians, or Alaskan natives. Don't ask questions with racial implications. For example, "Did you ever receive public assistance?"

Age

The age discrimination legislation protects people between forty and sixty-five. Any questions, therefore, that could easily lead to the determination of age should be avoided. For instance, do not ask, "How old were you at the time of graduation?" It is the more subtle questions, however, those that imply concern about age, that could provide the basis for a suit. Don't ask about:

- Ability to "keep pace." For example, avoid such questions as, "This is a very hectic place. Do you think you can keep up with it?"
- Age-related relationship. For instance, "How do you feel about working for a person younger than you?" Or, "How do you think you'll get along with the younger people here?"

Religion

It is illegal to discriminate on the basis of religion. Any questions, therefore, that inquire about religion or religious practices should be avoided. Examples of questions to be avoided are:

- Do you attend church regularly?
- Do you miss work in order to attend services on religious holidays?
- Are you active in any church groups?

National Origin

It is discriminatory to ask an applicant's lineage, ancestry, national origin, descent, parentage, or nationality. Any questions from which national origin can be deduced are inappropriate.

Do not ask for the applicant's birth certificate, baptisimal record, or naturalization papers. You can ask for proof of age if there is concern that the applicant is a minor or over 65. Unless needed, avoid asking the maiden name of a married female applicant. Here are examples of questions to be avoided:

- □ Inquiry into how applicant acquired ability to read, write, or speak a foreign language.
- □ Nationality of applicant's parents or spouse.
- □ Inquiry into the clubs, societies, or lodges to which the applicant belongs.
- □ Inquiry about the name and address of the nearest relative to be notified in case of accident or emergency. (Can ask for a person to be notified, but don't specify relative.)

You can ask:

- □ What languages the applicant writes or speaks fluently.
- □ Whether or not the applicant is a citizen of the United States.
- □ Whether the applicant is on a visa that will not permit him or her to work here.

Handicap

The Rehabilitation Act of 1973 states that discrimination against handicapped applicants on the basis of non-job-related criteria is illegal. In effect, you cannot discriminate against a "qualified handicapped" individual, that is, an individual capable of performing a particular job with reasonable accommodation to the handicap at the minimum acceptable level of productivity applicable to a nonhandicapped incumbent. Moreover, this same Act requires that government contractors, subcontractors, and agencies take affirmative action in the employment of qualified handicapped persons. Thus, contractors must make an effort to be sure that handicapped persons know about the open positions. Interviewers may find it helpful to obtain a list of national organizations serving the handicapped. They can be found in the *Directory of Organizations Interested in the Handicapped,* published by the People to People Committee on the Handicapped, 1146 Sixteenth Street, N.W., Washington, D.C. 20036. Avoid asking:

□ Questions about the handicapped candidate's height, weight, previous illnesses, or physical ability to handle the job.

You are permitted to:

□ Describe the nature of the job tasks to be accomplished, and then ask if the applicant believes he or she is capable of performing the task.

A helpful summary of key points is shown in Figure 31.

Retention of Interview Notes

The interviewer's primary defense against claims of discrimination are the interview notes. This is another good reason to take careful notes during the interview. The various Acts and laws concerning discrimination in hiring specify the duration of time that records must be kept. For example, the Age Discrimination in Employment Act of 1967 requires that employers keep records for one year on applications, test papers, physical examinations, and advertisements. Even for temporary jobs, applications must be kept for ninety days.

Applications and employment data for apprenticeship programs must be kept two years or the period of the successful applicant's apprenticeship.

How the Law Works

The agencies that enforce discrimination laws are empowered to initiate investigations of companies' employment practices. However, most often they respond to specific employee complaints of discrimination. When an investigation reveals that discrimination may have occurred, the agency will attempt to work out a voluntary solution with the employer. If these efforts fail, public hearings may be required.

If a hearing reveals that discrimination has in fact occurred, the company involved may be required to provide redress to the aggrieved party or parties. Redress may take

FIGURE 31.   Summary of interview guidelines.

Legal Guidelines (all applicants)

In accord with the latest EEOC legal requirements, organizations should consider revising their application forms, so that the following items are eliminated:

Race
Sex
Age (date of birth)
Marital status
Names and number of dependents
Name and/or address of any relatives
Job title and occupation of spouse
Height
Weight

In addition to these, it is illegal to discriminate in employment because of physical handicap or liability to military service. Inquiries in these categories should not be asked on the application or during the interview.

Following are some examples of discriminatory and acceptable inquiries:

Birthplace and Residence

It is potentially discriminatory to ask:

- Birthplace of applicant
- Birthplace of applicant's parents
- For a birth certificate, naturalization papers, or baptismal record

It is acceptable to ask:

- Applicant's place of residence

Creed and Religion

It is potentially discriminatory to ask:

- Applicant's religious affiliation
- Applicant's church or parish or the religious holidays observed

FIGURE 31. (*continued*)

Race or Color

It is potentially discriminatory to ask:

- Applicant's race

Age

It is potentially discriminatory to ask:

- Applicant's date of birth or age except when such information is needed to:
  - —maintain apprenticeship requirements based upon a reasonable minimum age
  - —satisfy the provisions of either state or federal minimum age statutes
  - —avoid interference with the operation of the terms and conditions and administration of any bona fide retirement, pension, or employee benefit program
  - —satisfy insurance requirements

Citizenship

It is potentially discriminatory to ask:

- Whether the applicant is now or intends to become a citizen of the United States or to inquire into any other aspect of citizenship

It is potentially acceptable to ask:

- Whether the applicant is in the United States on a visa that would not permit work here

National Origin and Ancestry

It is potentially discriminatory to ask:

- Applicant's lineage, ancestry, national origin, descent, parentage, or nationality
- Nationality of applicant's parents or spouse

Language

It is potentially discriminatory to ask:

- Applicant's mother tongue

It is acceptable to ask:

- Language applicant speaks and/or writes fluently

FIGURE 31. (continued)

- Language commonly used by applicant at home
- How applicant acquired ability to read, write, or speak a foreign language

Relatives

It is potentially discriminatory to ask:

- Name and/or address of any relative of applicant

It is acceptable to ask:

- Names of relatives already employed by the company
- Name and address of person to be notified in case of accident or emergency

Legal Guidelines (female applicants)

EEOC and the courts have declared that women must **not** be considered on the basis of any **assumed characteristics** generally attributed to females, nor may job opportunities be denied women on the basis of the physical requirements of a job, such as hours of work, weight lifting, and so forth.

Female applicants should not be asked questions about the following:

- Plans for raising a family
- Type of birth control used in family
- Number and ages of dependents
- Babysitting arrangements
- Occupation of husband
- Training or experience not expected of a male in a similar job, for example, typing ability for a chemist

the form of rehiring, back pay, early promotion, or whatever is relevant to the case.

In some cases, enforcement agencies may impose special rules for remedial action when companies are found lagging in antidiscrimination efforts. In cases under the Executive Orders, a company may lose its government contract.

Hypothesis Method as Deterrent

As the reader is now aware, the hypothesis method is designed to help the interviewer understand how the applicant behaves and functions and predict job behavior from past achievements. Since the goal of almost all employment assessments is to determine whether the individual can carry out the tasks and behaviors needed to successfully perform the job in question, historical data (except for knowledge-experience) in and of themselves are of no particular significance. The past is relevant only in the sense that it provides a means of predicting the future.

This point can be made clear by examining a classroom discussion. Imagine an interview demonstration in front of a class. Suppose the demonstration includes an interview of a fifty-year-old person, and the life area being explored is "years before high school." During the interview, the class is asked to write down hypotheses that emerge. Once the demonstration is over, hypotheses are solicited from the class members and are written on the blackboard. Now the "applicant" is asked the extent to which these hypotheses describe him or her *today*. Almost invariably, the applicant will indicate that about "80 percent describe me." If I ask those in the class who personally know the applicant if the recorded hypotheses are correct, they almost always say that the hypotheses correspond exactly to how the person really behaves.

Notice what has happened here. The applicant is talking about episodes in his life that took place thirty to forty years prior to the time of the interview, and yet the candidate, as well as those in the class who know the individual, indicate that the generated hypotheses describe the person *today*. How is that possible? One explanation, of course, is that many of our behavior patterns are set early in life and don't change much. But another more significant reason for this phenomenon is that the person is interpreting past events through current perceptions. When the applicant is asked, for example, what he has learned from an early school experience, he is not answering this as a ten-year-old child, but from the viewpoint of an adult today. In other words, the factual background that is being explored is the remote past; the hypotheses that develop from that past (in response to the self-appraisal question) explain how the individual functions right now.

It is not necessary, therefore, to explore and probe a person's personal life or areas that are illegal to learn what a person is like and how that person functions. As interviewers, what we are really trying to learn from the interviews is whether the person thinks, deals with people, is motivated, is knowledgeable in ways that will enable him or her to perform the job in question.

Another way to look at the role of historical data is that a person's history is simply an admission card to the interview. If the candidate's educational background or work history were not reasonably appropriate, the odds are small that the applicant would be in the interview situation. Once the applicant passes that initial screening and is reasonably qualified by virtue of knowledge and experience, it is not so important to probe for many more specific facts, but rather to understand *how* and *why* the facts already presented were accomplished. Self-appraisal questions and observations during discussion of legitimate topics allow the interviewer to describe how the person currently functions and performs. This should be the real test as to whether or not an applicant is suitable for the job. There is no reason for interviewers to feel handicapped in assessing candidates because of current laws and regulations about hiring practices.

A Word of Caution

Information provided in this chapter should help the interviewer gain an understanding of the current rules and regulations governing employment practices. However, the field is constantly changing. New court decisions add new interpretations to the law, and the law is frequently changed, particularly at the state level. Therefore, while this book can assist you in avoiding major discriminatory practices, we recommend that you consult your firm's legal staff to keep you current on the new laws and court interpretations of them. Other questions also may be directed toward the local department of labor or civil rights commission.

Summary

This chapter describes the various aspects of a candidate's background that interviewers need to avoid inquiring about. It is not so much that the inquiry *per se* is illegal, but that asking for such data could be the grounds to support a legal action claiming discrimination. These areas are race, sex, age, marital status, religion, national origin, and physical handicap.

It is indicated that the hypothesis method is a technique that will help the interviewer understand how the applicant functions *now*, today. It is this information, rather than data that are risky to inquire about, that should be the basis of the hiring decision. Interviewers need not delve into illegal areas to make an effective assessment of a candidate's qualifications.

Interviewers are cautioned to check with local human rights commissions, since laws are changing and also vary from state to state.

CHAPTER 16

Improving Interviewing Skills

The evaluation interview model and the approaches outlined in this book were designed to make interviewing both effective and easy. However, as with most activities requiring technique and skill, practice is necessary before one is able to use them with ease and grace. Thus to become proficient in assessing others, the manager will need to practice the evaluation model format and, in particular, focus on three techniques—asking self-appraisal questions, employing restatement, and recording hypotheses.

Need for Feedback

In order to learn how you are progressing in your interviewing, it is necessary to get feedback about what is being done right and wrong. It is only after hearing an interview that mistakes become apparent and corrective action can be taken. It is recommended, therefore, that those managers who wish to develop good interviewing skills use a tape recorder. Helpful feedback through tapes can be acquired either by taping an actual interview or through role-playing practice sessions with friends or business acquaintances.

Tape Recording of Actual Interviews

If managers want to listen to themselves in a real interview, they can accomplish this easily and much will be learned.

The interviewer should tell the applicant that the interview is being recorded. It is unethical to tape the interview without the applicant's approval. The candidate will usually accept the idea if the interviewer provides some valid reasons for the taping. Here are two examples.

INTERVIEWER: I'm working on developing my interview skills, so if you don't mind, I'd like to tape our discussion so that I can play it back later.

INTERVIEWER: I can't possibly remember all the things you're going to be telling me, so rather than try to take notes, I'm going to record our discussion. Is that all right with you?

Place the recorder out of sight, either on the floor or behind the desk, so that the applicant does not see the recording mechanism operating. If only the microphone is on the desk, the applicant soon forgets that the tape recorder is on, and the interview proceeds in the usual fashion.

Use a checklist for self-criticism. When listening to the tape play back, focus on the interviewer's ability to follow the evaluation model. It is also helpful to analyze which hypotheses were developed during the interview and which were missed. In Appendix B, a feedback checklist is provided so that the interviewer will have a guide in criticizing his tape.

Recording Role-Playing Practice Sessions

A second way in which the tape recording can be used to develop interviewing skill is to have a friend or business associate play the role of the applicant. This method has the advantage of being less stressful than the real interview, and it can also be worked into a short time period, such as a lunch hour.

One procedure that has been effective for many executives is for the interviewer to team up with someone else who is also interested in improving his or her interviewing skills. Each manager interviews the other for approximately ten minutes, limiting the discussion to one or two interview areas—high school and college, for example. While exploring each area, effort should be made to concentrate on opening the area with a broad-brush question, listening, asking self-appraisal questions, and weaving in relevant tested questions.

When one of the interviewers completes an area or two, the tape can be played back for analysis. The feedback checklist provides a good basis for making this critical review.

It is not essential that an entire interview be taped in order to practice interviewing. Once the sequence of steps for conducting the discussion in an area is mastered, the entire interview becomes easy to manage.

Apart from taping, one of the best ways to learn how to evaluate others is to conduct a number of interviews. The interviewer can practice the interview plan and revise it from time to time to find the most comfortable sequence of topics. Again feedback is important for maximum learning. Managers should make a point of discussing their assessments with others who may have interviewed the same candidate. If all interviewers of any given applicant devise a strengths and limitations balance sheet, along with a numerical rating on both qualifications and potential, such comparisons will help improve selection accuracy and also provide excellent feedback to the interviewer. Use of the two-on-one interview provides an excellent opportunity to observe others interviewing, and also to have your own techniques critiqued.

Interviewing is not difficult and can be stimulating and challenging once the interviewer is confident in the interviewing role. The evaluation model and techniques outlined in this book should substantially help the interviewer-manager approach the interview in a comfortable and relaxed manner. Eventually, of course, each interviewer may want to develop a personal system and structure for an interview, but, in the meantime, the model provides a foundation from which to start.

Summary

To become proficient in assessing others, the manager must practice the evaluation model by focusing on the techniques of asking self-appraisal questions, employing restatement, and recording hypotheses. Those managers who wish to develop interviewing skills can check on themselves by tape-recording actual interviews or role-playing practice sessions with friends or business associates. When playing back the tape, focus on the interviewer's ability to follow the evaluation model and to develop hypotheses.

APPENDIX A

A List of Tested Questions

The following chart is arranged so that the reader can easily find questions that are appropriate for use in any given life area. In addition, the columns at the right will help the reader identify questions that are likely to yield information about one or more of the four basic factors:

- **I** Intellectual factor
- **M** Motivation factor
- **P** Personality factor
- **K** Aptitude or knowledge factor

Thus, the reader who is obtaining relatively few inputs about intellectual functioning should select some questions from the I column and weave them into the next interview. The interviewer should not try to build an interview around these questions. They are offered only as a resource from which a few may be drawn for application in the tested questions step of the evaluation model or for ideas for the broad-brush questions of the campus interview model. Usually some experimentation is necessary before the interviewer evolves the most productive repertoire of tested questions.

	Probable Hypothesis			
	I	M	P	K
I. Years Before High School				
Did anything occur during those years before high school that you are particularly proud of?	x	x		
As you look back on those earlier years (before high school), was there anything you learned that you see carrying over to your adult life today?	x	x	x	x
During those years before high school, were there any activities you particularly enjoyed, apart from those in school? What was there about doing _____ that made it appealing?		x		
In your earlier schooling, let's say before high school, were there any natural talents or abilities you displayed that your teachers or parents commented about? What meaning, if any, do they have in your work success today?	x		x	
II. High School				
What degree of difficulty did you encounter in making your grades in school?	x	x		x
What were you thinking about during those high school years—as to what you wanted to do when you got out in the workaday world?		x		
What did you enjoy doing after school?		x		
What would you say you learned from your high school experiences that you see being carried over to your adult life today?		x	x	
III. College or Other Studies				
What do you believe is the basic meaning of a college education?	x	x		x
What do you think is the most valuable contribution it will make to your life?	x			x

	Probable Hypothesis			
	I	M	P	K
How did you view the importance of grades in college?		x	x	
What led you to choose _____ College?		x		
What prompted you to pick _____ for your major subject?	x	x		
If you had an opportunity to do your college years over, what might you do differently? Why?		x		
What subjects did you do best in? Why?	x			x
What subjects did you do poorest in? Why?	x			x
What was there about the subjects in your major that made them appealing?	x	x		
What did you learn from your extracurricular experiences that you see helping you today as an adult?	x			x
What motivated you to seek a college degree?		x		
What elective courses did you take? Why did you choose these particular ones?	x	x		x
If you had any part-time jobs while in school, which one or ones did you find most interesting? Why?		x		
What would you say is the most important thing you learned from your college career?			x	x
There is an opinion that student involvement activities infringe too much on valuable study time. What do you think about this?		x	x	
IV. Work Experiences (summer and full-time)				
What changes have you ever made in your approach to others in order to become better accepted in your work setting?			x	
What kind of people do you like to work		x	x	

	Probable Hypothesis			
	I	M	P	K
with? What makes them pleasant to work with?				
What kind of people do you find it most difficult to work with? What is there about them you would like to change?		x	x	
In your last job, what would you say were the main drawbacks to pursuing that kind of a job as a career?		x		x
Starting with your last job, would you tell me about any of your achievements that were recognized by your superiors?	x			x
Can you give me an example or two of your ability to manage or supervise others?			x	x
What are some things you would like to avoid in a job? Why?		x		
In your previous job, what kind of pressures did you encounter?			x	
What would you say is the most important thing you are looking for in an employer?		x	x	
How do you feel about travel? On the average, how many nights a week would you be willing to be away from home?		x		
What are some of the things on your job you think you have done particularly well or in which you have achieved the greatest success? Why do you feel this way?	x	x	x	x
What were some of the things about your last job that you found difficult to do?	x			x
What are some of the problems you encounter in doing your job? Which one frustrates you the most? What do you usually do about it?		x	x	
How do you feel about the progress you have made with your present company?		x		
In what ways do you think your present job has developed you to take on even greater responsibilities?	x		x	x

	Probable Hypothesis			
	I	M	P	K
What would you say was the most, or least, promising job you ever had? Why do you feel this way?		x		
What has been your greatest frustration or disappointment on your present job and why do you feel this way?		x		
What are some of the reasons that are prompting you to consider leaving your present job?		x		
What are some things you particularly liked about your last job?		x		
Most jobs have pluses and minuses—what were some of the minuses in your last job?		x		
Do you consider your progress on the job representative of your ability? Why?	x	x		x
What are some of the things about which you and your supervisor might occasionally disagree?			x	
How do you feel about the way you or others in the department were managed by your supervisor?			x	
In what ways has your supervisor helped you to further develop your capabilities?				x
What are some of the things your boss did that you particularly liked or disliked? Why did you feel this way?		x	x	
How do you feel your boss rated your work performance? What were some of the things he indicated you could improve upon?	x		x	x

V. Military Career

What, if anything, would you say you learned from your military service?			x	x
I know a number of appeals are often made to keep people in the service; how did you evaluate the situation—leaving versus staying in?		x		

	Probable Hypothesis			
	I	M	P	K
How do you feel about the military's authority structure?			x	

VI. Reactions to the Job and Company

	I	M	P	K
What do you see in this job that makes it appealing to you that you do not have in your present (last) job?		x		
How do you evaluate our company as a place to build your future?		x		
I know you don't have a good perspective of this job yet—not being in it—but from your present vantage point, what would you say there is about the job that is particularly appealing to you?		x	x	x
What would you say might not be highly desirable?		x	x	x
What is it that you are looking for in a company?		x		

VII. Goals and Ambitions

	I	M	P	K
Where do you see yourself going from here? You may not have any particular goal at this time, but if you do, what might you be thinking about?		x		
What is your long-term career objective?		x		
What do you think you need to develop yourself in to be ready for such a spot?	x		x	x
What is it you have going for you that might make you successful in such a job?	x		x	x
What are some things you would want to avoid in future jobs? Why?		x	x	x
Do you have any particular salary goals or targets? [If the candidate describes some, ask why he or she arrived at them.] What makes you think you will be able to earn that kind of income in _____ years?	x	x	x	x
What kinds of job or career objectives do you have?		x		

	Probable Hypothesis			
	I	**M**	**P**	**K**
Who or what in your life would you say influenced you most with regard to your career objectives?		x	x	x
Can you pinpoint any specific things in your past experiences that affected your present career objectives?		x	x	x
What are your salary expectations? What do you consider as fair salary progression from date of employment on?		x		
How does your family feel about your career plans?		x	x	

VIII. Self-Assessment

	I	**M**	**P**	**K**
What would you say there is about you that has accounted for your fine progress to date?	x	x	x	x
We've talked a lot thus far about your education and work experiences, but how about yourself—your other strengths and weaknesses? What might be some of the good qualities or traits you possess?		x	x	
How about the other side of the coin? Apart from knowledge or experience, what traits or qualities do you think could be strengthened or improved upon?		x	x	
What would you say are some of the basic factors that motivate you?		x		
What kinds of things do you feel most confident in doing?	x		x	x
What do you feel somewhat less confident about doing?	x		x	x
What are some of the things you are either doing now or have thought about doing that are self-development activities?	x	x	x	x
In what way(s) do you think you have grown most in the past two to three years?	x	x		x
Can you describe for me a difficult obstacle you have had to overcome? How did you	x	x	x	

	Probable Hypothesis			
	I	**M**	**P**	**K**
handle it? How do you think this experience affected your personality or ability? (The second and third questions usually are answered without asking.)				
How would you describe yourself as a person?	x	x	x	x
If you had your life to live over again, what things would you do differently?		x		x
What do you think are the most important characteristics and abilities a person must possess to become a successful _____? How do you rate yourself in these areas?	x	x	x	x
Do you consider yourself a self-starter? If so, explain why.		x		
What things in life that you have been asked to do have you found to be the hardest?	x	x	x	x
What would you consider to be your greatest achievement to date? Why?	x	x	x	x
What things give you the greatest satisfaction?		x		
What things frustrate you the most?			x	
How do you usually cope with them?			x	x

IX. Leisure-Time Activities

	I	M	P	K
What do you enjoy doing in your off hours?		x		
What is there about _____ that is appealing to you?	x	x	x	
What do you like to avoid getting involved in during your off hours?		x	x	
Are there any talents you possess that are used during your leisure time that you have not been able to apply in a work situation?	x	x	x	x

APPENDIX B

Interviewer's Feedback Checklist

	Yes	No
1. If small talk was used, did it put the applicant at ease?	___	___
2. Did the small talk seem manufactured or was it natural and directly related to the interview situation?	___	___
3. Did the interviewer open each area with a broad-brush question?	___	___
4. Was the broad-brush question in any way circumscribed so as to limit the applicant's response? For example, "Tell me about your college career and how you did academically."	___	___
5. Did the interviewer interrupt the response to the broad-brush question (for instance, with a question about what was being said)?	___	___
6. Did the interviewer make meaning out of the applicant's response to the broad-brush question by asking self-appraisal questions?	___	___
7. Did the interviewer use		
restatements?	___	___
open-ended questions?	___	___
silence or pauses?	___	___
acceptance?	___	___

8. Did the interviewer play down the applicant's
   shortcomings?   ____ ____

9. Did the interviewer give positive feedback (sincere compliments) from time to time?   ____ ____

10. Was the interview more conversational than a
    question-and-answer session?   ____ ____

APPENDIX C

Developing Behavioral Specifications

Job Title _____ Salary range or grade level _____
Location of Position _____

Knowledge-Experience Factor

What does the candidate have to know about or how to do in order to perform in the job?

_____
_____
_____
_____

What particular kinds of experience are absolutely necessary for effective performance on the job?

_____
_____
_____
_____

Motivation Factor

What should the applicant like to do (enjoy doing) to enjoy working in this job?

_____
_____

_____

_____

Is there anything the applicant definitely should not dislike doing?

_____

_____

_____

_____

Any goals or aspirations that are essential the candidate have?

_____

_____

_____

Any unusual energy demands in the job (long ours, constant travel, and so forth)?

_____

_____

_____

_____

How critical is overt drive? Must the incumbent push over, through, or around many obstacles?

_____

_____

_____

_____

Personality Factor

Any critical/essential personality qualities (decisive, action-oriented) needed for success in this job?

_____

_____

_____

How must the incumbent handle stress or pressure?

_____

_____

_____

What kind of interpersonal behavior is required in the job, if any?

Up the line _____

_____

Peer level _____

_____

Down the line _____

_____

Outside firm (customers) _____

_____

Intellectual Factor

Any specific intellectual aptitudes necessary (for example, math or mechanical)?

_____

_____

_____

_____

How complex are the problems to be solved? What must the incumbent be able to demonstrate he or she can do intellectually?

_____

_____

_____

_____

How should the candidate go about problem solving (off the top, cautious, deductive, and so forth)?

_____

_____

_____

_____

APPENDIX D

Suggested Agenda for a Two-Day College Recruiter Workshop

This outline provides suggested topics and time allocation for training nonprofessional recruiters, that is, managers who may be interviewing on campus without much prior experience in conducting such interviews.

First Day—Morning Session

Introductions and objectives of workshop. Skill as well as knowledge.

Role and function of the recruiting coordinator. How college relations staff will coordinate and integrate the recruiting effort—an overview of the organization's recruiting system, procedures, programs, and requirements.

Resource information. Materials, handouts, review of company benefits, and unique aspects of company.

Recruiting from a placement director's viewpoint. A visiting college placement director from a campus at which the organization recruits discusses the placement office philosophy, methods of operation, and student attitudes and reactions.

Questions applicants ask most frequently. Suggested responses are provided.

First Day—Afternoon Session

Selection criteria. Company groups describe qualities of a successful candidate for their particular program, and selling points about their specific operations.

The campus interview. Participants view film, "The Campus Interview,"[1] and hear presentation on the use of company's evaluation forms and after-interview procedures.

EEOC guidelines. Organization policies and methods of implementation. Do's and don'ts.

Panel discussion and question-and-answer period. Individuals experienced in recruiting (from the firm) relate their experiences and answer questions.

Second Day—Morning Session

Interviewing for assessment. A comprehensive presentation of effective interview techniques for campus and secondary interviews at company locations. Training focuses on specific interview procedures as well as development of necessary skills to carry them out.

Second Day—Afternoon Session

Interviewing for assessment (continued). The afternoon is devoted to role-play practice sessions in which participants practice conducting thirty-minute campus interviews, as illustrated by film on first day.

Summary and concluding remarks.

---

[1] A twenty-minute film describing how to conduct the campus interview. Professional Educational Materials Division, Drake-Beam & Associates, Inc., 277 Park Avenue, New York, N.Y. 10017.

APPENDIX E

A Sample Format for Requesting Transcripts

Date: _____

To: Registrar

_____

Please furnish a transcript of my record, at their expense, to:

(Your Company Name and Address)

_____

_____

_____

☐ I am a candidate for a _____
                                   (degree)

_____   _____
          (major)   (expected graduate date)

☐ I received a _____

_____   _____
          (major)   (date)

Signature: _____

Address: _____

_____

Selected Reading

Banaka, W.H. *Training in Depth Interviewing.* New York: Harper & Row, 1971.

Cabrera, J.C., and E.A. Galiskis. "A Participative Executive Search." *Personnel,* January–February, 1974.

Citti, R. "When You Say 'No' to Job Applicants: How to Avoid Charges of Bias." *Supervisory Management,* Vol. 18 (1973), pp. 2–6.

Decker, P.J., and E.T. Cornelius. "A Note in Recruiting Sources and Job Survival Rates." *J. Applied Psychology,* Vol. 64 (1979), pp. 463–464.

Drake, John D. *The Campus Interview,* New York: Harcourt Brace Jovanovich, 1981.

Drake, John D. *Counseling Techniques for the Non-Personnel Executive.* New York: Harcourt Brace Jovanovich, 1974.

Fear, Richard. *The Evaluation Interview* (2d ed.). New York: McGraw-Hill, 1973.

Fear, R.A. *The Evaluation Interview* (3d ed.). New York: McGraw-Hill, 1978.

"The Headhunters Come Upon Golden Days." *Fortune,* October 9, 1978.

Jackson, T. *Interviewing Women: Avoiding Charges of Discrimination.* New York: Executive Enterprises, 1976.

Lopez, F.M., Jr. *Personnel Interviewing: Theory and Practice* (2d ed.). New York: McGraw-Hill, 1975.

Rogers, J.L., and W.L. Fortson. *Fair Employment Interviewing.* Reading, Mass.: Addison-Wesley, 1976.

Stanton, E.S. *Successful Personnel Recruiting and Selection.* New York: AMACOM, 1977.

Ulrich, L. and D. Trumbo. "The Selection Interview Since 1949." *Psychological Bulletin,* Vol. LXIII (1965), pp. 100–116.

U.S. Dept. of Labor. *Questions and Answers on OFCC Testing and Selection Order.* Washington, D.C.: U.S. Government Printing Office, 1974.

Wagner, R. "The Employment Interview: A Critical Review." *Personnel Psychology,* Vol. II (1949), pp. 17–46.

Wright, O.R., Jr. "Summary of Research on the Selection Interview Since 1964." *Personnel Psychology,* No. 22 (1969), pp. 391–413.

Index